Stories and Customs of the

SHERPAS

As told by
Ngawang Tenzin Zangbu,
Abbot of Tengboche Monastery

Stories and Customs of the

SHERPAS

As told by
Ngawang Tenzin Zangbu,
Abbot of Tengboche Monastery

Edited by Frances Klatzel

Translation assistance by Ang Kanchi Sherpa
and Passang Thondup Sherpa

Fourth Edition

Mera

Mera Publications
Kathmandu, Nepal
2000

Published by Mera Publications and the Sherpa Cultural Center, March 2000.

ISBN No. 99933-553-0-5

First edition, Khumbu Cultural Conservation Committee, May 1985.
Second edition, Khumbu Cultural Conservation Committee, September 1988.
Third edition, Mandala Book Point, July 1995.
Fourth edition, Mera Publications, May 2000.
Second printing, Mera Publications, January 2001.

Mera Publications Pvt. Ltd.
PO Box: 38, Kathmandu, Nepal
Phone: 428752
Email: francesk@wlink.com.np

Drawings: Ekaram Maharjan and Norbu Lama
Design: Format Graphic Studio, Kathmandu. Phone: 428572
Printing: Format Printing Press, Kathmandu. Phone: 422160

Table of Contents

Editor's Acknowledgments

Thank you to the following for their assistance and advice with the previous editions of this book: Passang Thondup Sherpa, Ang Kanchi Sherpa, Matthieu Ricard, the Banff Crag and Canyon press, Nepal Lithography, a private donor, and the many people who have offered encouragement and suggestions.

Rinpoche and I would like to thank the following for their past support of the Sherpa Cultural Center at Tengboche: the American Himalayan Foundation, Canadian Everest Society, a private donor, Cultural Survival, the Department of National Parks and Wildlife, and the late Professor Christoph von Furer-Haimendorf.

Further acknowledgements for fourth edition:

For this new edition of "Stories and Customs of the Sherpas," I would especially like to thank Ani Jampa Chokyi (Helly Pelaez Bozzi) for corrections to the phonetic spellings of Tibetan and Sherpa words and names. Mattheiu Ricard corrected and contributed to the glossary. Though every effort has been made to verify and correct any errors in the previous three editions, any errors are the responsibility of the editor. Lhakpa Norbu Sherpa and Kathy Butler reviewed the final manuscript and made valuable suggestions. Tsering Sherpa helped with photographs and typing corrections. Anil Raj Shrestha of Format Graphic Studio contributed considerable creative energy to a new design of the book. Thank you to all.

Most importantly, I would like to thank Tengboche Rinpoche for the opportunity to work with him on the Sherpa Cultural Center for several years. While compiling information for the museum and this book, our conversations often digressed to aspects of philosophy, psychology and spirituality that revealed the significance of the Sherpa rituals, traditions, and symbols, and unveiled other ways of seeing the world. This opportunity has enriched my life, for which I will always be grateful.

Many thanks (tuches) to all my Sherpa friends in Khumbu and Kathmandu who have so generously welcomed me into their homes and lives for the past twenty years. I would also like to thank family and friends in Canada, Nepal and other countries for their unwavering support and encouragement.

Frances Klatzel
Kathmandu, June 2000

Royalties from the sale of this book help support Sherpa cultural projects in Solu-Khumbu, especially those that promote cultural education classes and that do not ordinarily attract the attention of donors.

Thank-you for purchasing this book. Any donations for these projects would be most gratefully accepted, please contact Mera Publications for more information.

Introduction

Visitors from many countries come here to see and to climb Jomolangma, Mt. Everest. Often you want to know about the culture of our Sherpa people. Therefore, we have made this little book of cultural information to help you understand our way of life.

We originally made this book through the Sherpa Cultural Center project at Tengboche monastery in the Solu-Khumbu district of east Nepal. The Center was built because so many people are interested in Sherpa culture and stories. I wanted to make a book about the Sherpas' heritage. Khumbu is changing and people may forget their culture and stories.

Before the 1950s there were only Sherpa people in Khumbu. Today Tengboche is on the main trekking route to see Mt. Everest. Often in the spring and fall, about one hundred trekkers come here daily.

If we start preserving our Sherpa culture here, the idea will spread to other places. As well, it is very important to help the people and the government develop the country.

People from within and outside Nepal, for example, His Majesty's Government and also Sir Edmund Hillary, have helped and advised in the continuing development of Tengboche.

The Sherpa Cultural Center has been for visitors and for the long-term benefit of the Sherpas. At Tengboche, we are working on four kinds of projects.

- The school provides opportunities for learning traditional Sherpa studies and skills that are important to the preservation of our heritage.
- The Tengboche Development Project is promoting much needed and appropriate development schemes such as water and sanitation. We also have a small hydro-electricity plant.
- The library preserves rare Sherpa books, has the main books from each sect of Tibetan Buddhism, and makes Tibetan and foreign texts available for study.
- The first museum completed in 1988 had two floors. Upstairs we tried to explain as much as possible about the religion of the Sherpas. Downstairs exhibits were about Sherpa history, customs, and culture. Though many things are similar to the Tibetans, the museum especially showed those distinctive to the Sherpas. After fire destroyed Tengboche's gompa in 1989, the upper floor of the museum served as the main prayer-room of the monastery for three years and the museum was partially dismantled. We are presently working to build a new better, more suitable building, and refurbish and expand the exhibits.

For all Nepal and the Sherpa and Nepali people, we plan to have the school and the Cultural Center here for the future.

Chapter One

The Sherpas and the Khumbu Valley

The Sherpas and the Khumbu Valley

First about the Sherpas; who we are

Our name, Sherpa, means "easterner" because we came from Kham in eastern Tibet. One of the first persons to come to Khumbu came by way of Rolwaling valley and Tashi Labtsa (pass). He opened this valley so that other people could come to settle. Later many families came from Tibet over the Nangpa La (pass).

This person came to Khumbu from Kham-Salmo-Gang (east of Tibet). His clan was called Thimi, and his name was Phachen. When he came to Tibet, the people asked where he came from— "the east part of Kham." That is how the name Sher-pa, meaning east-people, came to be.

For 600 years, people have migrated from Tibet to these mountain valleys in Nepal. There was a time of great unrest in Tibet when many lamas, their families, and followers left their homes looking for new places to live. They settled in the mountain valleys of northern Nepal. These places came to be called Yolmo (Helambu), Langtang, and Khumbu.

Now we live in the Solu-Khumbu district, Sagarmatha zone of Nepal. We live in the highest places. In Khumbu, we number about 3,200, with another 30,000 Sherpas living in the Solu, Langtang, Helambu, and Rolwaling valleys.

Gradually, some people emigrated from Solu-Khumbu district to other areas: Sankuwasawa, Helambu, Langtang, Ilam, and Charicot. Later, too, some moved to Sikkim, Assam, and Darjeeling in India. Because they spread from here and because their language is similar, they are all called Sherpa.

The Sherpa language (a dialect of Tibetan), literature, history, and philosophy came from old Tibetan religious books.

About this Khumbu Valley

To tell a short story about Khumbu: here is the highest mountain in the world. We call it Jomolangma, because a goddess, one of the five sisters of long life, resides there.

Guru Rinpoche, the founder of Tibetan Buddhism, hid the Khumbu and other Himalayan valleys for future times when people would need them as sanctuaries. He described Khumbu in religious books as a valley surrounded by snowy peaks. Following directions in these texts, some people moved into these areas of northern Nepal.

There are two main areas where the Sherpas live. In the old times, they called the upper Khumbu valley, Khumbu-te, and the lower Solu valley, Shorung. The upper Khumbu valley looks like a flower bud about to bloom. Pharak, also called Khumbu-me, in the middle of the Dudh Kosi gorge is shaped like a channel. Shorung is shaped like a lotus on the water. Solu-Khumbu district lies in the northeastern part of this peaceful country called Nepal, near the Tibet border.

When we first came here, snow covered the Khumbu Valley and the glaciers here were much bigger. Hence, the first settlements were down near Lukla. As the snow and ice gradually melted, people moved up to Tashinga, and then eventually started villages at Khumjung and Pangboche.

The main villages in Khumbu are Khumjung, Khunde, Thamichhok, Namche, Pangboche, and Phortse. Most Sherpas have a home in one of these villages but often stay for the summer monsoon in huts at the high pastures.

Our Religion and Culture

In Solu-Khumbu, the most common sect of Tibetan Buddhism is the Nyingmapa, the oldest tradition. Sherpa and Tibetan lamas taught this religion to the people and organized the communities.

These Sherpa and Tibetan *ngagpa* (lay lamas) brought teachings from Tibet to Khumbu that were from books hidden by the founder of Tibetan

Buddhism, Guru Rinpoche. Lamas called *tertons* are incarnations of Guru Rinpoche who rediscovered these hidden teachings. *Ter* means "spiritual treasure" in Tibetan. A lama named Rigdzin Godem found some of these books, the *Chang-ter*, hidden in northern Tibet. The other lama, Nyatak-Nyung, found the Lho-ter in southern Tibet. The *terton*, Terdak Lingpa found the books and wrote the texts used in the Sherpas' *pujahs*, religious rituals.

As more people came to Khumbu, traditions started that helped to unite the villagers and to protect the valley. Daily life revolves around each village *gompa* (temple). Closely tied to Buddhist beliefs are our daily activities of farming, herding and trading. Since the 1950s we have worked for tourists and earned fame on climbing expeditions.

About Nepal

According to our religious texts, we live north of the center of the world. In the center of the world, Lord Buddha attained enlightenment at a place called Dorje Den, or Boudhgaya, in northern India. North of Boudhgaya is Nepal.

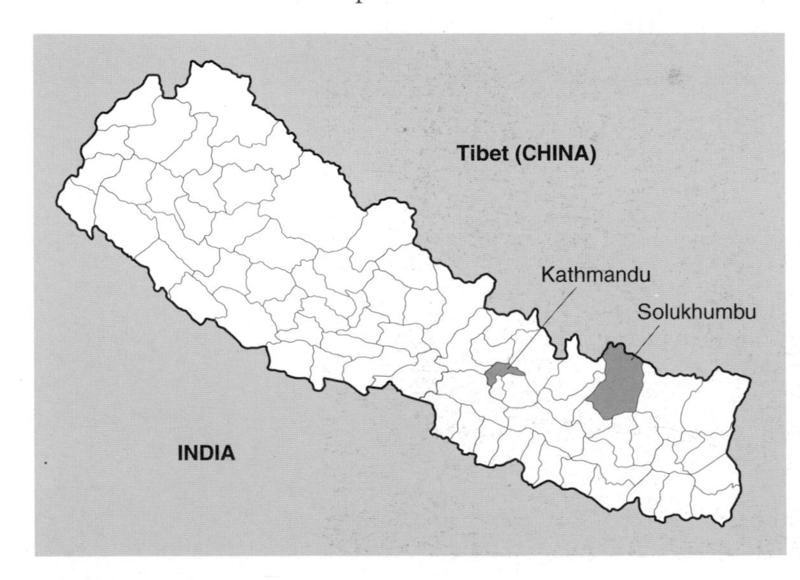

In Nepal, especially near the Tibetan border, there are high valleys and a long line of many mountains. In Solu-Khumbu district, we have Jomolangma. North of the Humla district of west Nepal, is a special mountain called Kang Rinpoche (Kailash). Other northern areas also have special mountains.

Nepal is the most special place in the world for Hindus and Buddhists. Here, are many important books, statues, and places. Many places are important pilgrimage destinations for Sherpas.

In the Kathmandu Valley there are several sites including Phawa Shingu, called Swayambu in Nepali, a *stupa* (*chorten* in Sherpa / Tibetan) built by nature, and Chang-Khasher, called Boudha in Nepali. Near Kathmandu is Namo-Boudha, where the Buddha in an incarnation as King Nyendup Chenbo, offered his body to a starving mother tiger. Pashupathi, called Shiva Jiz by the Hindus, honors a deity also revered by Buddhists as the action form of Phakpa Chenrezig, the deity of compassion.

Far to the southwest of Kathmandu is the Buddha's birthplace, Lumbini. Nearby was the palace of his father, the King Sudodhana.

In Nepal, there are many high reincarnations. The famous monarch, Gyalpo Sekey Kocha Chen was the father of an incarnation of the goddess Green Tara, and was himself a reincarnate who treated the people well and affectionately.

Stupas above Namo-Boudha

Prayer wheels in old Tengboche gompa

Chapter Two

Sherpa Buddhism

Sherpa Buddhism

Our Buddhist ways aim at generating spiritual energy for the benefit of all beings. Religion is a way of life, unifying all aspects of our lives.

Traditionally *ngagpa* (married lamas) in each village conduct ceremonies and teach religion. Our beliefs came through the oldest sect of Tibetan Buddhism, the Nyingmapa, which started when Guru Rinpoche established Buddhism in Tibet over 1260 years ago.

From long ago, people living in Nepal's mountain valleys have practiced the Buddhist religion. Guru Rinpoche's books state that if the people do not lose their religion, these valleys will remain peaceful. The four sects practiced by these people are the Nyingmapa, Sakyapa, Kargyupa, and Bon-po (pre-Buddhist sect). As well, Tibetans, who are now refugees living in Nepal and India, practice the Gelukpa sect.

The Nyingmapa sect uses all three forms of Buddhism: Hinayana to improve one's character, Mahayana to think about others, and Vajrayana to follow a short cut to spiritual liberation.

We describe the power of nature as protective deities. For example, Jomo Miyo Lang Sangma, a goddess, resides on Jomolungma (Mt. Everest). Qualities such as wisdom and compassion are also depicted as deities. Envisioning these deities helps us to concentrate while meditating.

Prayers to the deities may influence important events and daily activities. Offerings and prayers accompany weddings, funerals, and births. We may do prayers for the benefit of an individual or a community.

To practice their Buddhist faith, our people build *gompas* (temples). There are now about 3,000 gompas in villages, monasteries, or sacred sites in Nepal.

About Lord Buddha and Buddhism

Briefly, let me tell you about Lord Buddha. The Buddha was born from his mother's right side at a place called Chal near Lumbini in southwest Nepal over 2500 years ago. Sheltered from any human misery until the age of 29, he then left his princely life to seek a solution to humanity's suffering. As an adult, he meditated for six years beside a river at a place called Chewa Narenjana.

Then several years later, while meditating near Boudhgaya in northern India, the Buddha attained enlightenment, the fulfillment of complete awareness and compassion in his mind. The god Brahma asked him to teach this all encompassing faith. The Buddha first taught this path to spiritual growth in Benares (Varanassi) and continued teaching until his death 45 years later.

Buddhism flourished in India for almost 1700 years. It also spread to South Asia, China, Central Asia, Japan, and the Kathmandu Valley. Guru Rinpoche brought Buddhism from India to Tibet over 1260 years ago where it took on a unique character and eventually split into several different sects.

Religion in the Mind

The purpose of religion is to perfect our minds. It protects our character from being polluted, which is why religion is so important in our culture. There are many stages in our religion to help make our minds useful. First, to improve one's own character, there is Hinayana. After, when you are ready to think about others, there is Mahayana. Even higher thinking is called Vajrayana.

Our own minds cause happiness and unhappiness. There are two rivers to follow in our minds: the Shunya and the Karuna. The first deals with perception and the emptiness or non-reality of all things. The Karuna deals with compassion. After these two aspects of our minds have attained perfection as maha-shunyata and maha-karuna, and their two currents have merged to become indistinguishable, one then attains Sangye Kyi Sa, Buddhahood.

Three Schools: Hinayana, Mahayana and Vajrayana

The Buddha's teachings formed a school of Buddhism called Hinayana, which aims at the individual's enlightenment or liberation. Later, the Buddha taught a few followers the Mahayana, which aims to attain liberation for all beings. For many years, the Buddha traveled teaching the Sutra, both Hinayana and Mahayana. The Buddha foretold that Guru Rinpoche would come to teach another approach to Buddhism, the Vajrayana.

The three schools of Buddhism are often explained as paths up a mountain. Hinayana leads to the base of the mountain. Here one sees one road and one method. Mahayana is the long gentle road that winds around the mountain to its summit. In this school, one sees many roads and decides to take the gradual path. In Vajrayana the practitioner looks beyond the roads and takes the most direct, but risky, route straight up the cliffs to enlightenment and liberation at the summit of the mountain.

There is also a story about a poisonous plant in a beautiful garden. The student of Hinayana, upon seeing the plant, is most likely to leave the garden altogether. A Mahayana follower, realizing that small amounts of poison may also act as a medicine, will examine the plant. Afterwards, a practitioner of Vajrayana comes along. Believing that poisons often only appear to be dangerous, he eats the whole plant, quickly attaining Dewachen, Amitaba's pure land, a phase on the way to liberation and enlightenment.

Guru Rinpoche

Guru Rinpoche: The Founder of Tibetan Buddhism

Guru Rinpoche, also called Ogyen Rinpoche or Padma Sambhava, was born in a lotus flower in Ogyen (in the west of India) about 1260 years ago. The Ogyen King Indra Bhuti was himself an incarnated bodhisattva and had spent all of his wealth on religious deeds. He went to the sea to ask for more wealth. There, he found the child on a lotus flower and adopted him.

Eventually, all the king's wealth, property, and power passed on to the boy, who ruled the country for some time. This young ruler gave all this up to pursue religion with many high teachers. He meditated and taught Vajrayana in Ogyen, India and in Nepal, until eventually he was invited to Tibet.

The King of Tibet was Trisong Detsen. Together, he and Guru Rinpoche built Samye, the first monastery in Tibet around the year 779 AD. Guru Rinpoche called many Indian Buddhist teachers to join him to help teach the Sanskrit language (of early India) to the bright Tibetan children.

In many places in Tibet, Guru Rinpoche also taught the Vajrayana School of Buddhism. He taught some of this knowledge directly to the people. He instructed his students to write other teachings in *ter*, (special books) that they hid in rocks or the earth, or made invisible. Guru Rinpoche predicted that a time would come when religion would become loose and confused, when people would break laws, disobey lamas, and break vows of government and religion. Even in the gods' place, it would be heard that on earth everything is in chaos. Guru Rinpoche foretold that certain people, reincarnations of his disciples, would find the *ter*, these hidden books. The collection of these books is the Rinchen Terdzo, and the people who found them are the *tertons*.

Phakpa Chenrezig

Guru Rinpoche knew that in the future, there would be a war in Tibet and the Tibetans would have to leave their land. He foretold that the mountains would be refuges for these times. Khumbu, Rolwaling, and Khenpalung are the three hidden valleys in this region.

Phakpa Chenrezig: the Deity of Compassion

Phakpa Chenrezig has many different forms, each with a different name. Each main *ter* (book by Guru Rinpoche) mentions him.

The name Phakpa is a term of respect, Chenrezig indicates that he is the aspect of the Buddha's complete compassion. One of his forms is called Jigten Wangchuk or Thuje Chenpo in Tibetan, and Arya Lokeshvara in Sanskrit, because he is said to come from the Buddha's thought.

A Buddha needs Khyenpa (bidwaan in Sanskrit) wisdom, Tsewa (karuna - Skt.) compassion, and Nüpa (shakti -Skt.) spiritual powers to help enlighten and liberate all animate beings. *Maha-karuna,* complete compassion, is the most essential of these qualities.

"Mani" is the *mantra* (chant) for Phakpa Chenrezig. This very important word helps us become compassionate and achieve Phakpa Chenrezig's power to attain enlightenment. All Tibetan people are part of Phakpa Chenrezig and know the mantra "mani" without being taught.

Many Tibetan lamas are incarnations of Phakpa Chenrezig because of his blessing of Tibet. The Dalai Lama is an incarnation of Chenresig, as was the first Buddhist king of Tibet, Srongtsen Gampo. Through his incarnations, Phakpa Chenrezig gives direct teachings and pujahs that have been continuous and practicable. Phakpa Chenrezig also gave blessings in India, so that some people there became thubthob, (bodhisattvas - compassionate reincarnates) capable of performing miracles.

Jomo Miyo Lang Sangma

The action form of Phakpa Chenrezig is called Lhachen Wangchuk, or in Sanskrit, Maha-deva meaning the great deity. He is very powerful from having maha-karuna, complete compassion. Because we worship him here in Nepal, people know, like, and want to help our small country. Both Hindus and Buddhists honor this deity.

About Jomolangma (Mt. Everest)

Here is the highest mountain in the world. I could see Jomolangma from Tibet and from near Darjeeling in India. The book, Khenpalung Lamyig, says Jomolangma is here in Khumbu.

Jomolangma is the name of the mountain. Jomo Miyo Lang Sangma is the name of the resident female deity. She is a mother goddess and one of the five sisters of long life.

According to a religious story, father Lhola Tebu and mother Menthang had five daughters. Tashi Tseringma resides on Gauri Shanker and gives long life, Jomo Miyo Lang Sangma gives food, Tekar Dosangma gives *wangdup* (good fortune), Chopen Dinsangma gives wealth, and Thingi Shelsangma gives telepathic powers.

Traditionally, Jomo Miyo Lang Sangma is a deity of humans, so many pilgrims used to go to Rongbuk to see her. Now, people, from all over the world, come to see the abode of Jomo Miyo Lang Sangma, Jomolangma, from Khumbu.

Jomo Miyo Lang Sangma rides on a red tiger. This goddess is very pretty; she is orange and bright looking. She wears a garland of many kinds of flowers around her head and robes of many colors. In Jomo Miyo Lang Sangma's right hand is a long bowl of food and in her left a mongoose that spits wealth.

About Khumbu-Yul-Lha, the Guardian Deity

Khumbu-Yul-Lha

The name Khumbu comes from Khumbila Tsen Gylapu, the guardian deity of the Khumbu Valley. The name Khumbila is short for Khumbu-Yul-Lha, which translates as Khumbu-country-deity. Khumbila protects the people, religion, and land of the Khumbu. He is one of the twenty-one deities in Tibet that Guru Rinpoche subdued and converted. His mountain home, Khumbila is above Khumjung and Guru Rinpoche describes this mountain in his book Khenpalung Lamyig.

Khumbila's father is Tashi Palwoche and mother is Lho Menthang Ghongma. Khumbila and Nangpa Gothaya are among his father's students. The deity residing on Tamserku, Tamosermu, is Khumbila's wife.

Phortse village with Kantega and Tamserku in background

Chapter Three

The Khumbu Country

The Khumbu Country

Long ago in Tibet and Khumbu: The Creation of the Land

Phakpa Chenrezig, the deity of compassion, created the land of Tibet. According to tradition, when the Buddha was about to leave this earth, Phakpa Chenrezig asked him to stay longer. Buddha replied "my time is finished."

"But there are still many beings on earth to enlighten."

"That is your responsibility, mine is finished," replied the Buddha, giving to Phakpa Chenrezig the responsibility to enlighten the Tibetans.

Khumjung

In the book Mani Kabum, Buddha foretold that a country of snowy hills and lakes would be drained and dried. Later, from a hillside in Tibet, Phakpa Chenrezig saw all the land of Khumbu and Tibet covered by water. Snow or forests covered all the hills. Many beings lived in the forests and the water.

Phakpa Chenrezig meditated; to drain the water from this land, to send all the beings to Dewachen, and to bring religion to the people who would inhabit this country.

Another text the Chang-ter, foretold that a big war would destroy everything in Tibet. At that time, religious people would have to flee to high mountain places described by Guru Rinpoche. The Khumbu valley is one of these places. Its full name Khumbu-Khangki-Rawa translates as "Khumbu-surrounded-by-snowy-mountains".

Guru Rinpoche hides the Khumbu

Guru Rinpoche came first. Long ago, Guru Rinpoche was meditating in a cave in Hallashey, a place south of Solu, called Dubphug Mara Tika in religious books. He flew from here to a cave above Khumjung, called Akarphug. Here he spent three days. At this time there was snow all around. After destroying or converting the bad spirits, Guru Rinpoche foretold that this Khumbu Valley would be a *beyul*, a sanctuary from the troubled outside world.

Later, a king of Tibet, Trisong Detsen, had a wife, Margyen. Although she was queen, she was not allowed to live with the king for three years. She was very angry and disappointed. Margyen lived with a dog during the day and with a goat at night. Almost ten months later, she bore a son with a dog's mouth and a goat's skull. The queen hid the child from the king while it was young. When the boy was older, Guru Rinpoche said to send him away, but the queen was embarrassed that her son might be seen. So Guru Rinpoche magically flew the son to a valley called Khenpalung, southeast of Khumbu.

In this valley, Guru Rinpoche and the son made a palace and had yaks, naks, and fields. After the son, Khyikha Rathö, had lived there for three years, Guru Rinpoche returned and said that he had to go to another place. As Guru Rinpoche and Khyikha Rathö climbed out of the valley, Guru Rinpoche sent clouds and rain to hide the palace so they could not return. Guru Rinpoche hid Khenpalung for the future, to be one of the beyul he described.

Khyikha Rathö could not find his way back to the valley and had to come through Amphu Labtsa to Dingboche. He made his way down to Dun Latso, then Monjo, where he planned to build a big palace on top of the rock. Khyikha Rathö wondered if a flood coming down from the mountains would wash away the palace. So, the son of the angry queen moved down to Dholaghat, near Kathmandu, where he died. With the main symbols of evil expelled by Guru Rinpoche, the Khumbu valley became a *beyul.*

Khenpalung is a hidden valley where people will age slowly. It has not yet been opened to people and sits at the center of a ring of hidden valleys, like the center of a *mandala* (symbolic map). There are many ways to get to it from all around. Khumbu is one of these routes.

Khumbu, the Hidden Valley

Guru Rinpoche, after hiding this beyul within the mountains, instructed his students to write books describing the locations of the valleys and how to get to them. The students were to hide these books in rocks and the earth and make them invisible. In hard times during their future lives, these students would find and use the books.

Guru Rinpoche

The text found by Rigdzin Godem, reveals that southwest of Shripal, two weeks and one day walk away, sits the Khumbu valley surrounded by the mighty Himalayas.

The text Gongpa Zangthal describes Khumbu as a valley in the middle of the Himalayas that is a good place to live. Khenpalung Lamyig is a book of instructions on how to get to Khenpalung and how to travel to Khumbu from Tibet. It also describes Khumbu as a valley shaped like a horse facing towards the west. The body of the horse has two villages, Khunde and Khumjung.

Phachen opens the Hidden Valley

Long ago, Khumbu was all covered by snow and the glaciers were much bigger than they are now. The snow first melted from south facing slopes such as on Khumbila.

Gradually the snow and ice melted and the hillsides grew forests and grass. The Khumbu started first at Khumjung, below Khumbila. To the north of Khumbu is Gothaya and Cho-oyu. To the northeast is Jomolungma, to the south is Kantega, and to the west are Kwongde and the Tashi Labtsa.

When the time came to open the beyul for the people, there was a man who while meditating during the night could dissolve into *osal* (clear light). During the day, he could dissolve into the rocks. Generations later, one of his descendants, Phachen, went from Kham-Salmo-Gang to Shripal, which is north of Khumbu in Tibet. Phachen worked his way to Kyabrog, then by Sallung to Rongshar, through Rolwaling, and over Tashi Labtsa to Khumbu. Along the way, he destroyed many bad spirits.

Phachen came and stayed at a cave below Namche called Trilbi-phug. At that time, this place was very wild and full of spirits guarding the beyul. The spirits collected lots of wood to kill Phachen by lighting a fire at the entrance of the cave. He cut a hole through the rock (with this spiritual power) and fled from the cave to Phurte, near Thame.

Phachen had enough spiritual power to subdue the spirits causing problems for the newly arrived settlers in the area. Once while he and his wife, Chemi Aphe, lived near Jorsalle, Phachen was away on a trip to the south. Phachen heard his wife's voice and left a mark on a stone. This omen meant that the two of them would stay together.

Another time when Phachen was first in Khumbu, he was down near Chauri Kharka collecting wild animals from the forest for good luck. He told Chemi Aphe to tie them up but not to make any noise for it would scare them away. While tethering the hundredth animal, she was tired and sighed. Her sigh scared the animals and Phachen could not catch another animal. Thereafter, in Khumbu, people believe that it is impossible for one family to keep more than one hundred animals.

Phachen's descendants, the Paldorjie clan, started and dedicated Khunde, the first village in Khumbu. His descendants spread throughout Khumbu and Solu, as there were not many other people around.

The Kiranti Rai

Shortly after Phachen arrived in Khumbu, there was a fight between brothers of a Kiranti Rai family in east Nepal. One of them ran away from Panch Pokhari, east of Khumbu, over Amphu Labtsa and down to Dingboche, where he built a house. Eventually, he moved down to Dong-lhamzo (near Tengboche). After building many houses, the Rai moved back down to his homeland. Now, only Sherpas live here.

The opening of the Nangpa La

Once a man's dog ran off following a deer. Kira Gonbo Dorje followed them over the Nangpa La into Khumbu and opened the pass. The route was very difficult at first, but gradually the snow melted down and now it is much easier to cross between Khumbu and Tibet.

Most of the Sherpa clans and Tibetan people came to Khumbu over this pass. It became the main route between Tibet and Khumbu.

Chapter Four

Religion in the Khumbu

Religion in the Khumbu

Lama Buddha Tsenchen

Two generations after Phachen, Buddha Tsenchen was born at Mohang, a small hermitage on the slopes of Khumbila. He lived there and at Gurmje nearby. During this time, the deity Khumbila visited Buddha Tsenchen every day. Usually, the lama would burn a bit of juniper as a welcoming.

One day, they were discussing finding a salt mine in Khumbu. Buddha Tsenchen's wife, curious and jealous as to what was happening, burst in interrupting their conversation. It was a bad omen and since then it has been hard to converse with Khumbila so the salt conversation has not been resumed and no one has found a salt mine in Khumbu.

Lama Sangwa Dorje

Buddha Tsenchen had three sons: Lama Sangwa Dorje, Ralpa Dorje, and Khyenpa Dorje. All three sons became lamas. They taught religion, started gompas in the villages, and organized the communities.

Lama Sangwa Dorje

Lama Sangwa Dorje strengthened the Sherpa's religion and communities by starting many traditions. This son of Lama Buddha Tsenchen was born about 350 years ago in Khumbu low on Khumbila, between Mohang and Tashinga. Even when Sangwa Dorje was small, he was very powerful and respected.

During this time, Khumbu was a *beyul*, a remote hidden

valley. The scattered settlements in Khumbu Valley had no permanent leaders until the three sons of Lama Buddha Tsenchen started the village gompas and organized the communities. Sangwa Dorje was in Pangboche, Ralpa Dorje in Thame and Khyenpa Dorje in Rimijung.

Lama Sangwa Dorje went to study religion in Tibet and Helambu. Later he came back to Khumbu to teach the people. He went to study at a place in Tibet called Kochak, between Tingri and Sakya. His teacher, Rigdzin Jigdral Zangpo, was the fifth in a succession of teacher-disciples since Terton Ratna Lingba found the texts hidden by Guru Rinpoche. Jigdral Zangpo had been told that a reincarnation, with many kinds of knowledge, would become his disciple.

Jigdral Zangpo taught Sangwa Dorje that a student must follow the instructions of his *lama* (teacher), his *yidam* (personal deity), his *khando* (goddess of wisdom, dakini), and his *cho kyong* (defender of Buddhism). It was essential to follow and obey all the instructions in a book before studying it thoroughly. Under this famous lama, Lama Sangwa Dorje also studied the Chang-ter (books hidden by Guru Rinpoche), the Drowa Kundol, and learned how to make *mandalas* (symbolic maps) and *torma* (ritual offering cakes) for use in prayers.

Lama Sangwa Dorje visited many pilgrimage places in Tibet and went on many religious retreats. During these retreats, he practiced meditation, eventually attaining a state of spiritual enlightenment. While at high levels of thought, Lama Sangwa Dorje was able to perform many miracles.

When Sangwa Dorje came back to Khumbu, he had a hermitage at Namkar Dzong above Dingboche, and two meditation caves on the mountainside above Pangboche called Sengi Duphug and Yon Phug. First at Namkar Dzong he practiced body meditation. Later, he moved to practice speech meditation at Senge Phug and then returned to Namkar Dzong to practice mind-heart meditation. It was at Yon Phug that he attained enlightenment.

A local Sherpa legend says that when Lama Sangwa Dorje was meditating in the caves, a yeti brought him food and water each day. When the yeti died, Sangwa Dorje placed its scalp and hand in Pangboche gompa.

Sangwa Dorje visited the hidden valley of Khenpalung three times and went to Helambu, where he shared teachings with another lama, Thubten

Pawo. When he visited pilgrimage places in Tibet he meditated at a place above Rongbuk called Mani Khang where there was only a flat place to sit. Here while he reached high levels of thought, he saw rainbows on top of Jomolangma and realized Guru Rinpoche's meditation state, Sangdog Palri, which is a level of enlightenment. While at this high level of meditation, he flew to the top of a pinnacle where he left footprints in the stone.

Later, Lama Sangwa Dorje founded Pangboche gompa. The village looks like a *phumba,* a sacred vase with the gompa sitting right in its middle. In the gompa is a *ku* (statue) of Gonpo Sungjon, an aspect of the protector deity, Maha-kala. This statue is believed to have told Lama Sangwa Dorje where to build the gompa. Sangwa Dorje preserved special Sherpa books, the Ratling Cho-kor.

Once in Pangboche gompa, he hung his *cho-go* (shawl) on a sunbeam and another time flew from Khumbu to the north side of Everest. Lama Sangwa Dorje left footprints in stone in many places and even his dog's tracks on a rock near Pangboche. While meditating at Tengboche, his foot slipped, leaving a deep mark on the stone where he sat. He predicted that someday there would be a very good monastery here.

Lama Sangwa Dorje helped sick people and gave them medicines so the Medicine Buddha protected him.

When his teacher, Jigdral Zangpo, passed away, Lama Sangwa Dorje went back to Kochak to make a statue of Jigdral Zangpo and teach his son, Norbu Wangyal. Lama Sangwa Dorje stayed there to be the local lama.

After several years, Lama Sangwa Dorje visited Cho-phug, just below Rongbuk. Here he taught his many students and followers. Lama Sangwa Dorje passed away in Cho-phug. His heart, eyes, and tongue did not burn in the cremation and were placed in a *ku-dung* (reliquary).

The people of Pangboche did not have any relics of Sangwa Dorje, so they went to Cho-phug to retrieve some. The story is that they got the gompa caretaker drunk so that he just put the lock on the bolt without latching the gompa door. That night the Pangboche people went in and took the *ku-dung* containing Lama Sangwa Dorje's relics. They brought it over the Nangpa La and installed it in the Pangboche gompa.

Lama Sangwa Dorje's legacy continues long after he passed away. Since his time, several village lamas of Pangboche have been his disciples and the villagers of Khumbu have followed the Ratna Lingpa teachings and traditions with which he inspired them.

Lama Sangwa Dorje's fifth reincarnation was Ngawang Tenzin Norbu, the founder of Rongbuk monastery who encouraged the establishment of Tengboche monastery.

About other Lamas and more Gompas

Several years earlier, about the same time as Buddha Tsenchen was at Mohang, there was a gompa at Lhowar, near Khumjung.

Ralpa Dorje, another one of Buddha Tsenchen's sons, established Thame and Kyobrog (upper Thame) gompas about 380 years ago. The third son, Khyenpa Dorje, 10 years later built Rimijung gompa across from Phakding. A powerful lama in Phortse, Rigdzin Choki Gyaltsen, founded a gompa and had several students.

Lama Serwa's clan built Tashi Tongmon gompa in Junbesi and other small gompas and hermitages around Solu about 350 years ago. At this time, several lamas, specially Jatang Choying Rangdol in Thame, brought most of the Chang-ter (hidden texts of Guru Rinpoche's) to Khumbu after studying near Kyirong in Tibet.

All these lamas, called *ngagpa*, studied, and practiced Vajrayana. Having not taken any particular vows, some of them had families.

Junebesi gompa

Sherpa Prayers

The Sherpas' prayers to the small deities all around are called Lha Chudub. Sherpas say these prayers because it is important to think before starting any work. For

Lha Chodub

example: if you keep yourself and your house clean, you will have hardly any sickness, and if you pray, the deities will help with the good things you want to do. Then, even if your enemies are wishing bad luck to you, they will not be successful.

During the third month, Sherpas pray for good crops. In the sixth month, they do Yerchang to bring luck to their herds and animals. Sherpas also do prayers when they build a new house or if they go away for a long time or distance.

There are different kinds of deities to worship when you are alive and others at death. Shitro are prayers to two kinds of deities at once. The Shiwa are kind, pleasant deities; the Trowo are ugly, wrathful, and fierce. The Thodol describes these deities. Shitro may be done for someone while they are alive, as Shitro Srog-ngo, or as part of their funeral rites.

The purpose of Shitro is to purify and gain merit for the person's spirit. Even if a person has not done meditation in their lifetime, Shitro still cleanses the spirit. For example: if gold is dirty and black, but is heated and cleaned, it comes out bright and shiny. Our minds are not stable, because we see things as good and bad. Our desires and dislikes are like dirt on a window. Through prayers, meditation, Shitro rituals, and trying to keep the balance in our thoughts, we can cleanse our "windows" so that we can perceive ourselves more clearly.

Nyungne is a special pujah to Phakpa Chenrezig. We do this pujah on special days such as when the Buddha went to *Dewachen* (liberation). It is performed for the benefit of villages or in one's own home. The villagers, *anis* (nuns), or *tawas* (monks) gathered together will eat one meal the first day, but cannot eat meat or drink *chang* (local beer). The next two days, they cannot eat, drink water, swallow saliva or talk. On all three days they do prostrations and pray.

Chapter Five

Sherpa Traditions

Sherpa Traditions

About the Sherpa Clans (*ru*)

Ru is a Sherpa word meaning bones. The male line transmits the *ru* (bones) and so the father's lineage determines one's clan membership.

Four main clans originally came from Kham, in eastern Tibet, to Solu-Khumbu: the Thimi, Thakthowa, Chawa, and Lama. Each clan gave rise to several brother-clans and continuous migration has brought many new clans into the area.

Most of the Sherpa clans came to Khumbu over the Nangpa La (pass). Only the first arrivals, the Thimi, came via Rongshar and Rolwaling.

The Paldorjie clan gave rise to the Salakha, Dhag Shingto, Kambache, and Goparma. A clan called Michen-topa in Kham, but Thakthowa here, gave rise to the Gole, Gartsa, Pinasa, Pankarma, Sharpa Penagpa, and Shari-topa brother-clans. From the Lama clan came the Serwa and Gombawa brother-clans. The Chawa remained a single clan that originated from a lama and his family that came from Tibet about 360 years ago.

Other clans that came to Khumbu more recently are Chu-sharwa, Murmin, Lhukpa, Nawa, Shangku, Zongnagpa, and Mendawa.

Since then, many people have continued coming from Tibet and other parts of Nepal. Newars, Chetris, Tamangs, and blacksmiths (Kamis) have moved up from the lower valleys of Nepal. Though these people are from different areas and religions, they often pray to the Buddha while here in Khumbu.

Each clan has its own deity and ways of doing pujahs. Sherpa custom does not allow marriage between members of the same clan or brother-clans.

Upper Khumbu people usually pray to Gonpo Maning, a deity who is sometimes male, at other times female. Solu people worship Gonpo Chagshipa, who has four arms. Different clans pray to other deities. Paldorjie prays to Bhari Lhatsen, Nawa to Tawache, Chu-sharwa to Lobuche, Sherwa to Arkamche, Thakthowa to Lung-kyung Bhari, Mendawa to Kharte Gyalu, Chawa to Chagpe-chagkung Karpo, and the Gartsa clan to Zhamte Chen. There are also special deities worshipped by the Shorung clans. The deities represent the different manners by which the clans do *pujahs*.

Sherpa Weddings

There are several stages to a Sherpa wedding. Sodene is the asking or the engagement. Demchang is the establishment of a proper agreement. Trichang sets the year and month of the final ceremony; Pechang is the consultation that sets the actual date. Zendi is the final ceremony where the woman comes to live with the man.

For the Sodene, the local village lama is called to the man's house to perform a pujah, Serkym. The man's relatives all come for food and then go to the women's house to ask. They take *chang* (rice beer) specially made for the occasion. If the woman and her parents agree, then anytime from one month to two years later, a special day is set for the for the Zendi ceremony. The families call the *ngagpa*, the village lama, to perform the pujah for the Zendi.

The Zendi begins with the Lhapsang pujah that starts at the man's house where the family gives *tso* (special cones of cooked rice) and displays the *khorma* (a flag representing the wheel of life). All of his relatives are called to drink and eat. Then they move to the bride's house, taking more special chang that they present to her parents and relatives. While presenting the chang, they pray to

Zendi

Guru Rinpoche and present *kattas* (white ceremonial scarves) to all of her family.

Then a man from each family respectfully introduces the families and praises the house for good luck. The village lamas write this speech, the *mola*, especially for the occasion. It must be read by an experienced person.

The bride's family gives her presents and property that is their official inheritance to her. They choose several girls, who have both parents and good luck, to carry these belongings in the procession to the groom's home. On the way, the groom's relatives and neighbors meet the procession at certain locations to welcome the new couple and to present chang and kattas. This happens again at his home.

Then the singing and dancing starts. The girls carrying the property, the *kerme*, go with the couple and their close relatives for several days to have parties in the homes of the groom's relatives and friends. In between parties, neighbors and relatives bring scarves, chang, and money to the couple. On either the fifth or seventh day, the couple returns to the bride's home for a ceremony, the karma-lo, to keep some good luck at her parent's home.

Some of the Sherpas' Special Days

There are two kinds of Lhosar, the Tibetan New Year: Sonampa Lhosar and Gyalpo Lhosar. Sonampa Lhosar is celebrated in the twelfth Tibetan month by people who farm, because by the first month they are already busy in their fields. Religious people, officials, and business people observe Gyalpo Lhosar in the first month, usually February. The first fifteen days of the year commemorate *chötrul*, religious miracles, performed by the Buddha.

During each Tibetan month, on the eighth, tenth, fifteenth, and thirtieth days' people offer *tsog* (offerings) and *torma* (ritual cakes) and go on little pilgrimages. The eighth day of each month commemorates Sangye Menla, the Medicine Buddha. On the tenth day of each month is *Tse Chu*, when Guru Rinpoche returns to earth. The fifteenth day is when Opame, the Buddha of infinite light, visits and the thirtieth day is the Buddha's auspicious day.

As well, in all of the villages, there are other special times. Saga Dawa, the fourth month, is the Buddha's special month. The seventh day honors the birth of the Buddha. The fifteenth day commemorates the Buddha's enlightenment.

Drugpa tse shi on the fourth day of the sixth month observes the first day the Buddha taught. The 22nd day of the ninth month celebrates when the Buddha returned to earth after teaching his mother in the deity's place.

In each village, pujahs are done twice a year in the spring and autumn to protect the crops and fields.

Dumje Festival

Villagers celebrate Dumje from the seventh to the thirteenth days of the fifth month. The tenth day celebrates the anniversary of Guru Rinpoche's birth on a lotus flower. Another day commemorates when Lama Sangwa Dorje attained enlightenment.

Pujah *to Khumbila at Dumje*

Lama Sangwa Dorje started Dumje in Pangboche about 350 years ago. It serves as a religious and community duty to bring the villagers together. Each family has its turn to provide the festival for the village.

There were people around Khumjung and Thame then, but few in Namche. For Dumje, some people from Namche and Khumjung used to go to Pangboche, while the others went to Thame. After several years there came to be more people in these villages, so they built a gompa in Khumjung. At that time, a descendent of the great teacher Rigdzen Jigdral Zangpo was a lama living in Khumjung. He agreed to help establish this village gompa.

Eventually the Namche people quarreled with the Khumjung people, so they built a new gompa in Namche and started doing their own Dumje.

Dumje helps bring peacefulness and cooperation to the

community. In each village, eight families a year have a turn at sponsoring Dumje. Eventually everybody has a turn. To prepare for the festival, on the seventh day of the month, the year's sponsors hold a meeting and the next day they arrange all the cooking utensils and food. On the ninth day the Dumje *lawas* (sponsors), eight families from the village, begin giving rice to all the other villagers.

The next day is the Lhapsang pujah to worship Khumbila. On the thirteenth day, a lama blesses the villagers for long life.

Each village has its own style of doing Dumje. Now the villages of Pangboche, Khumjung, Thame, and Rimijung celebrate Dumje. Three days earlier, a similar festival, Tso-chhar, is at Kyarock. In 1995, the new settlement of Lukla started celebrating its own Dumje in the fourth month.

Dumje type prayers are done in Tibet, but giving rice, and food is only done in Khumbu, where it is possible because the communities here are small.

Special torma used at Dumje are made according to the mystic diagrams specified for the pujah called Thugdup Yang Nying Düpa.

About Sherpa Funerals

The *sem* is the mind of the person. The *loong* is the energy of their mind. After death the *loong* (energy) from the body leaves but still exists.

When a person dies, a lama is called to perform Phowa. The lama doing the Phowa must join his energy with that of the dead person to try to bring about good, positive energy for the deceased. He uses prayers and pulling the person's hair so that the spirit leaves via the head.

A person's body heat may leave from the soles of their feet, hands, eyes, ears, nose, mouth, or the top of the head. The spirit then follows in that direction. If the spirit leaves from the front or back passages, it will have a bad life in the future. After exiting via the nose or eyes, it may be animal or human, but departures from the head may lead to Dewachen. The lama doing the Phowa must be well practiced in meditation to try to send the spirit out through the head and prevent it from leaving via bad parts of the body.

A nun prepares relics

Later lamas sit by the body reading the Thoedol, instructions to the spirit on which path to follow in the after life. The lamas continue praying and offer *tsog* (offerings).

There are many different customs, but, usually, the body is kept for three days then taken to the cremation site. After being washed, the body is cremated as an offering to the deities.

Every seven days after the death, special prayers called Dun, are offered in the home of the deceased. Within three or four weeks, the prayers called Shitro are done. Depending on the finances of the family, these prayers last from three to fifteen days. A special altar of torma and tsog is erected. Every evening the family places *sur* (an offering of tsampa) on the fire's hot coals as food for the spirit of the deceased. The Bar-do is the existence or time and space between lives. By the end of 49 days after the death, the person's next life is determined and they may be reborn.

When a child less than eight years old dies, a special funeral called Len-chang torma is performed for the benefit of the child and its parents. Tormas and food pellets of tsampa are changed about every hour at each repetition of the prayers. The funeral lasts three to four days, but sometimes as many as fifteen.

Dung-chog is the pujah for high lamas. It appears to be similar to Phowa, but its meaning is different. Dung-chog is performed later so that the lama's mind and the energy in it can become disengaged. The energy goes to the deity's pure realm from which it may be reincarnated. The Dung-chog pujah helps to straighten the road that this energy must follow.

Yak pastures in the monsoon

Chapter Six

Everyday Life of the Sherpas

Everyday Life of the Sherpas

The Sherpa Language

The Sherpa language originated from the old Tibetan religious books. There are many different dialects used in Tibet. As well, words from other languages such as Newar, Nepali, Tamang, and English have gradually come into our speech. The Tibetan language from Lhasa has also changed since that time.

Our Occupations

Before 1959, most Sherpas farmed and traded with Tibet. The business with Tibet was usually for salt and wool. Today, most people work mountaineering, trekking, portering, or doing religious services. The old people spend some of their time saying whatever prayers they know, going around stone mani walls and village *lha-khangs,* and helping with their families.

Making rigi kur (potato pancakes)

Sherpa Food

Potatoes, buckwheat, and barley are traditionally the main foods in Khumbu. Except for items brought up by traders, Sherpa food is limited to crops that can grow at the cold, high altitudes of Khumbu.

Sherpas eat some Tibetan foods, such a *tsampa*

(roasted barley flour), and some Nepali food such as rice. Unique to the Sherpas are green vegetables that are cooked then fermented to keep, and *kyu*, a sour or salty porridge of many grains—corn, rice, millet.

The Sherpas grow potatoes, buckwheat, barley, turnips, and greens. Dairy products include butter, yogurt, and cheese. They purchase rice, lentils, corn, millet and fresh meat from down-valley traders at the market. Salt and dried sheep meat is obtained from traders coming from Tibet.

Houses

When the Sherpas first came to Solu-Khumbu, our houses may have been bamboo huts. Gradually they changed to being half stone, half split wooden logs. Eventually they became stone houses, and later with two floors. At present, there are even some three or four story hotels and houses. Windows have been the fastest changing part of Sherpa houses with the introduction of glass panes.

The design of the *lha-khang* (chapel) was brought from Tibet. In every home it serves as a reminder of spiritual matters.

Usually the houses had simple windows with an opening in a wooden frame that closed by a small door. The wooden lattice windows became popular in Khumbu when a Tibetan carpenter re-building Tengboche gompa after the earthquake in 1934 used this design of window. Sherpas copied this design, especially in their household lha-khang windows.

The Dress and Appearance of the Sherpas

Traditional Sherpa clothing is similar to that of Tibetans. Most of their hats were distinctive to Solu-Khumbu.

The basic garment of the Sherpas, the *chuba*, originated in the cold climate of Tibet. It is a warm ankle-length robe that is bound around the waist by a long sash. The chuba's upper

portion becomes a large pocket for everything from money to bowls. Unrolled, the sleeves extend beyond the fingertips.

In the past, chubas were made from strips of hand-woven woolen cloth. Originally they were the undyed white color of the sheep's wool from Tibet. Later we started dying the wool black or brown. On trading trips to Tibet, people often wore sheep skin chubas, jackets or pants.

Men pull their chubas up to knee length and often withdraw their arm from the right sleeve. Under the chuba they wear a jacket or shirt with a stiff high collar, a *todung*.

tho

Women wear a sleeveless chuba called an *ungi,* or a sleeved one called *tongok*. Over it they wear striped woolen aprons on their front and back which in the old days were the same length as their ungi. The corners of front aprons (*mahtil*) worn on festive occasions are often decorated with brocade patches.

Over festive clothes, women will wear a long coat (*ungi tangtza*) with panels of wool and brocade. A newer style of festive hat is the *tsering kingab*; a high-crowned brocade hat with four fur-lined flaps worn by both men and women.

In the old times, both men and women wore long hair braided and would around their head. Older men often wore a long sash wound around their head called a *tho*. This kind of headgear is worn by the god Khumbila. The *se-sha* is a flat hat worn by men on festive occasions. The women wore a small diamond shaped hat on the top of their head called a *mo-sha*. The *wa-sha* is a warm, cloth and fur hat worn by traders and yak herders.

shang-dzin

Traditional boots are made from wool cloth. They may have leather soles (*kho-dzin*) or wool cord soles (*shang-dzin*). *Lham* are very old style all leather boots worn by men only.

Over the decades, the dress has changed. Men usually just wear trousers and shirts but still wear their chubas on special occasions like visiting lamas, weddings, pujahs, and festivals. Women's clothing is still traditional, except the aprons are shorter and hairstyles have changed. Now, men, children and teenage girls wear clothing that is more western-style.

C. von Furer-Haimendorf

Woman wearing serki mendok *and* serki tiktik *(1950s).*

Jewelry

Sherpas purchase jewelry as an investment and often select it for its auspicious properties. Sherpas accumulate their wealth by purchasing these stones which they wear as necklaces or set in gold or silver jewelry.

The three main stones used in Sherpa jewelry are coral, turquoise and dzi. Coral (*churu*) probably came to Tibet from the Mediterranean via the silk trade. Turquoise (*yu*) is found in Tibet or imported from Persia. Wearing this stone brings good luck and is especially good for one's health. If worn while ill, turquoise often becomes darker, thus it is believed to absorb toxins from one's body.

The black and white *dzi* stone is very precious. The more eyes a stone has, the more expensive and auspicious it is. It may be a kind of agate, or a kind of bead, but science has yet to fully explain the dzi. One legend about the dzi declares that to find it, you must go at a certain time, to a certain area of Tibet where you may see caterpillars that look just like dzi. Then you must throw your dirty clothes over the caterpillars. They turn to stone and you can gather the precious dzi in the morning.

Unique Sherpa jewelry is the "flowers of gold" (*serki mendok*), worn over a woman's ears, and the necklace of gold plates (*serki tiktik*). Women wear these only at festivals and now they are rarely seen.

In the old days, both men and women wore simple earrings of turquoise and coral on a string through their earlobe. They also wore large gold or silver hoop earrings set with a turquoise.

The *gao,* also called *serki klaabo,* is a box, often of gold or silver, which holds prints and sacred objects. They are often decorated with precious stones and worn by women on a necklace of dzi and coral.

A *dablam* is a shrine-shaped box for protective prints, relics and religious medicine that people wear on a cord and tuck in one's clothing.

A *chapchap* is a very old style pendant that attaches to the shoulder of a woman's robe. At the ends of its strands are small tools and toilet articles.

Monk's Clothing

Monks and other religious devotees wear clothing in keeping as much as possible with the ancient Buddhist code. In the old days the religious books were written in yellow and red. In the Himalaya, the monks' garments are red instead of yellow and because of the cold climate, wool instead of cotton.

The equivalent of the ancient Indian upper garment is a shawl worn by all religious devotees over their left shoulder and under the right arm. Ngagpas wear an *arti*, a shawl with three wide bands; red, white and red, down its length. Monks and nuns wear a plain red shawl (*youlzen*).

There are two special types of shawls. Monks wear these over their other garments on certain days of the month. The *namjar* is made from 108 pieces of yellow silk. The *cho-go* is made of wool. Another garment is a heavy, woolen cape worn during long services in the gompa.

The lower garment is a skirt (*shamthab*) which is gathered in folds and held up around the waist by a sash. Monks who have taken the final vows wear a special skirt made of 10 pieces. The multiple pieces of monks' garments symbolize the tradition of receiving alms including little pieces of cloth from which to make clothing.

There have been several different types of clothing developed specifically in the Himalayan region. These include a sleeveless waistcoat, an embroidered vest for special days, and a long sleeved jacket. Boots are made from threads of wool, cotton, silk or metal.

The *ngagpa* (married lamas) used to wear *shamthab* (white robes) from the waist down; *kenjar*, a red sleeveless shirt; *oygen-pezha*, their hat, and an *arti*, a white shawl with wide red bands along each side. The younger students wore long hair, a chuba, like a long coat, and a red cotton shawl. Now, *ngagpas* continue to wear the arti for pujahs, but with a red or brown chuba.

There are different hats for monks, nuns, lamas and reincarnates. The *tse-sha* are the high crested yellow hats worn by all monks during special prayers especially offerings.

The traditional water bottle from which a monk was to rinse his mouth in the morning is now almost a formality. It is a small metal vessel, entirely hidden in a rectangular cloth bag that hangs from the front of his sash.

Reincarnate lamas wear a special hat (*pe-ring*). Some of the hats, especially those worn by lay lamas, are modeled after the hats of Guru Rinpoche.

Tengboche Rinpoche wearing a pe-ring.

Mani stones near Pangboche.

Chapter Seven

Religious Objects

Religious Objects

Prayer flag with loong-ta

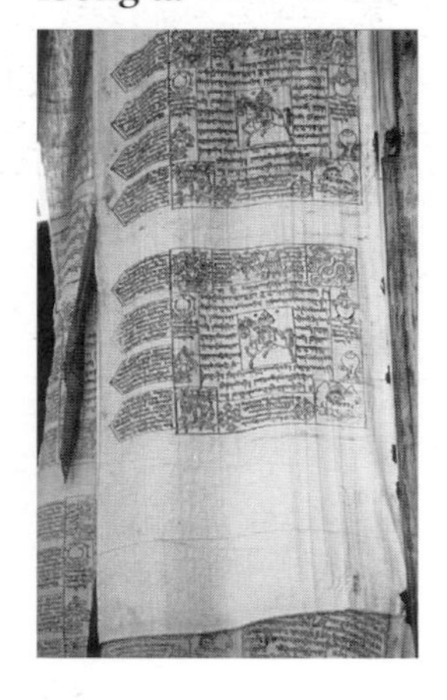

By invoking the blessing of Phakpa Chenrezig, these objects help bring peace into our lives. Used as part of our daily lives, religious objects help focus people's thoughts on Buddhist teachings and so bring about a good state of mind in people, to the benefit of everyone.

Religious objects help create harmony between our actions, body and mind. For when we gain merit first with our actions and body and then through our mind, the Buddhist teachings will come easily to us. So that everyone may understand them, religious objects have many explanations at these different levels.

Anyone may build a religious monument or object and so gain spiritual merit. The thoughtful offerings of those who made them are multiplied by each flutter of the prayer flag in the breeze, each turn of the wheel, each traveler's respectful gesture.

Prayer flags flutter in clusters on roofs or mountain passes, are strung across rivers and paths, or mounted on tall poles. The five colors of prayer flags signify the elements; yellow — earth; red — fire; green — wood; blue — sky or water; and white — iron. Printed on wood blocks, they often show the *loong-ta* (wind-horse), the swift bearer of prayers with the four protective animals, the tiger, snow lion, garuda and dragon, in each corner.

Mani stone

Mani stones are found near paths, temples, villages and homes. They may be carved with a single *mantra* (chant) or a complete prayer.

Mani wheels are hollow cylinders containing scrolls

printed with prayers. Each turn of the wheel by hand or water amplifies the prayers. Prayer wheels vary in size from 5cm to 5m in height.

Stupas (*chortens* in Sherpa) are the most numerous monuments in Buddhist areas. They represent the Buddha because he asked to have his ashes left in a stupa. Usually stupas contain offerings or the relics of important lamas. There are eight different designs of stupas.

stupa

The Library: Buddhist Religious Books

In the Buddha's time there were no books of his teachings. It was about 400 years later that disciples wrote down his teachings in the Sanskrit and Pali languages. These books were brought from India to Tibet where they were translated from Sanskrit to Tibetan. The suffix *gyur* in names of Tibetan books means translated.

The two main collections of scriptures are the Ka-gyur and the Ten-gyur. The Ka-gyur records the teachings and words of the Buddha as recorded by his disciples. *Ka* means Buddha's word and *gyur* means translated. From India, several books were brought to Gyanak in Tibet. Here Indian and Tibetan scholars translated the volumes from Sanskrit to Tibetan. Some books have been lost in their original Sanskrit and Pali. The Ka-gyur has about 108 volumes. It is usually shelved on either side of the *lha-khang* (altar). Sherpas have these volumes read often for many purposes: for rain for the crops, for less sickness and misfortune, for peace in the villages and so that in the future, we will all become like the Buddha.

The Ten-gyur of 226 volumes is a set of commentaries on the Ka-gyur written by the followers of Buddha. The Ten-gyur contains writings on literature, law, grammar, logic, rhetoric, history, medicine, painting, prayers, pujahs and astrology. In Solu-Khumbu district, there are about 8 sets of Ten-gyur.

The Boom consists of 16 books of 100,000 verses that are like a diary of the Buddha's thoughts.

Traditional book

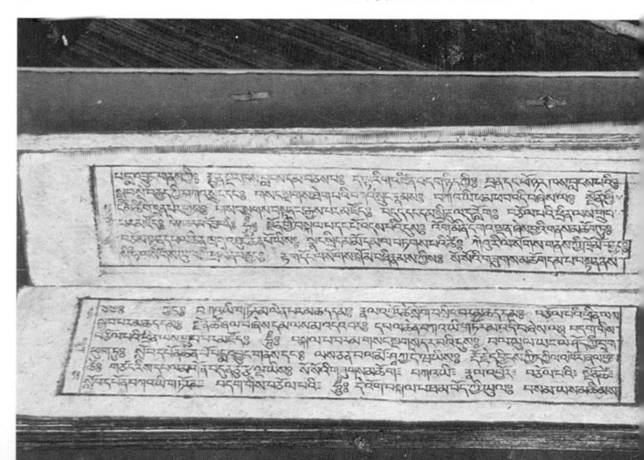

Many families have these books in their homes and have monks or lamas read them 3 or 4 times a year.

The Domang is a single volume that extracts the most important parts of the Ka-gyur. Most families have this book, which they read as often as once a month.

The library at the Tengboche Cultural Center also contains works from each sect of Tibetan Buddhism and the religious books used specifically in Khumbu.

The main religious books used specifically in Khumbu are the Ratling Cho-kor, Chang-ter Cho-kor, Jatson Cho-kor, and Minling Cho-kor. *Cho* means religion and *kor* means a variety of subjects. The old-style books, especially those used by the Sherpas, were handwritten and bound together along the long edge of the narrow pages.

The Tibetan books were traditionally printed from wooden blocks or hand-lettered onto long, narrow pages of local paper. The loose pages of each volume are stacked, wrapped in a square cloth, placed between two wooden planks and bound with a strap. In recent years, modern printing presses are used to produce Tibetan religious books so that now they are much more readily available and affordable.

Par (Wood-block Prints)

ku-par

Lamas give the prints to villagers who request them, usually at festivals or on special occasions, such as weddings or when they build a new house. They serve as aids in meditation, in rituals, and as protective icons for people and homes.

The prints are printed on *par-shing*, wooden blocks carved with the reverse image of the print. After ink is applied to the block, a piece of paper or cloth is pressed against the block.

Religious manuals precisely describe these images. Each detail of an image has meaning. The lotus shaped pedestals - on which the figures sit or stand -symbolize their spiritual birth. The deities' *mudras* (hand positions) and the emblems that they hold, express the gods' nature, function or activities. Different kinds of *par* have different functions.

Ku-par are pictures of the gods and of historic figures. These are usually displayed inside houses and used to help focus people's thoughts on spiritual teachings.

Srung—par are protective prints worn in a bag around a person's neck or put on the door of a house. They protect the wearer or household from illness, accidents and disasters. These prints usually show special kinds of *mandalas*.

Lok-par are prints that are burned or buried during ritual exorcisms. The most common kinds of Lok-par, *Meeg*, are prints of evil eyes.

Other special prints are used as prayer flags, displayed at weddings or placed under a dying person or a body about to be cremated.

Mandalas

Mandalas (*kyil-khor*) symbolize the order and harmony of the enlightened mind. They are geometric representations of the mind used as aids in the practice of meditation. Usually they show a square cross within circles with deities or Buddhas in the central focal point.

During meditation a practitioner mentally enters the mandala and visualizes the mandala in three or more dimensions with him or herself at its center. By achieving a state of spiritual unity with the Buddha or deities, the practitioner can absorb their energy and see the inherent order and unity of everything.

Special mandalas made of colored sands are made and used for rituals such as Mani Rimdu.

About Butterlamps

Lighting butterlamps gains merit, helping us on the way to *Dewachen*. They help us to see more clearly in this life and the next and help us let go of past attachments that keep us from Dewachen.

Pujah Instruments

The sounds of instruments used in *pujahs,* rituals, are offerings that bring us closer to the gods by making people happy, one of many small steps on the path to enlightenment. These sounds are said to be the counter-parts of the natural sounds of the body. Likewise, the *mantras* (chants) are believed to be connected to the natural sounds of truth in the human psyche.

The *nga* (drum) is used most as a tribute to Maha-kala, a guardian of Buddhism.

The *doong* (conch shell) is blown during offerings in prayers and calls the monks at all auspicious ceremonies. Its sound symbolizes the words of the Buddha who in a previous life was born in a conch shell.

gyaling

The *gyaling* is a Tibetan adaptation of the Indian flute. It is played in pairs during prayers to peaceful deities such as Dorje Sempa (Soul of the Thunderbolt) or the Tara (Savioress).

Zang-doong (long horns) translates as copper conch shells. Tibetans first used them to welcome *Atisha*, an Indian scholar, who came to teach Buddhism. These horns are always blown in pairs.

dhamaru and kagling

The *kagling* (trumpet) summons the gods and expels evil spirits. In the past they were made from thigh bones to symbolize impermanence and the expulsion of demons who hindered the establishment of Buddhism in Tibet. Today these instruments are made of metal.

The *dhamaru* (small drum) is held in the right hand and used to mark pauses between forms of worship. It is often used with the *dorje* or with the *kagling* and was also, in the past, made of bone.

bukchal *and* sil-nyen

There are three kinds of cymbals; one small and two large, distinguished by the size of their central boss. *Sil-nyen,* large cymbals with small bosses, are held vertically and used in offerings to peaceful deities. Those with large central bosses, *bukchal,* are held horizontally and used in prayers to fierce deities. The *ting-sha* (small cymbals) are used in offering rituals.

The sound of the *tylbu* (bell) is an offering to the gods that brings its user closer to awareness. A symbol of wisdom, it is held in the left hand while in the right hand is held a *dorje* (vajra). The *dorje* represents the indestructibility of the enlightened mind, the fitness of action and together with the *tylbu,* the enlightened mind.

dorje (vajra)

About Tying

Tying is a metal bowl on the *lha-khang*. Each set has seven bowls and some families may have two or three sets in which they daily offer water. The water seems worthless, so giving it is painless. It is very important in Buddhism that offerings are painless. From the water, we learn to give offerings to the gods. Then as we attain Buddhahood, we are willing to give our land, belongings or parts of our body to other people. Later it is less and less painful to give greater offerings.

Offering water in tying *in old Tengboche gompa.*

Chapter Eight

Tengboche Monastery

Tengboche Monastery

Tengboche monastery has been the heart of Sherpa culture since 1916. The first celibate monastery in Solu-Khumbu, it is a community of about 40 tawas (monks) under the leadership of the Abbot, Tengboche Rinpoche (Reincarnate Lama). Ten of the monks are away studying in India or Kathmandu. The school has about 25 students.

Tengboche sits east of Khumjung. From Tengboche one can see the abode of Menkyi Gyalmo Miyo-Langzangma (Jomo Miyo Lang Sangma on Jomolungma, Everest) and Ama Dablam to the east, Tamserku and Khangtega to the south, Tawache to the north and Kwongde to the west. Khumbila sits fat and beautiful in the middle of the valley. We are lucky to see Jomolungma, the most famous mountain in the world from here. The Dudh Kosi and Imja Khola rivers separate Tengboche from the other villages.

Below Tengboche are many big trees, but half way up are only a few large ones with many small shrubs. Throughout the spring, monsoon and fall, many different flowers bloom. *Masur*, the incense bush, covers all the high hillsides above Tengboche. If you walk in this area, the incense will help cure illness and ailments without any medicine. In this place, you forget everything, and feel peaceful and happy. This place is called Tengboche.

Founding Tengboche Monastery

Lama Sangwa Dorje's heel marks

Before, this was an empty place and the monastery site was covered by forest. Here, Lama Sangwa Dorje meditated, sitting on a stone where the gompa now is. While meditating, his feet slipped, leaving heel marks on the stone. Being able to see past, present and future, Lama Sangwa Dorje blessed this site and predicted that a very good monastery would be built here.

In 1914, a lama from Khumjung, Chatang Chothar, also called Lama Gulu, went to Rongbuk monastery on the Tibet side of Chomolungma. There he visited and studied with the lama Ngawang Tenzin Norbu. This high lama instructed Chatang Chothar to establish celibate monastery in Khumbu. Chatang Chothar worried about having enough money, but could not say anything, as it would be a bad sign.

Chatang Chothar (Lama Gulu)

Ngawang Tenzin Norbu understood his thoughts and said, "when you were Lama Buddha Tsenchen in a previous life, I was your son Lama Sangwa Dorje. So, because of this close relationship, you won't have any problems building the monastery and the future will be very good."

Then Chatang Chothar returned to Khumbu and talked with the Sherpas about where they should build the monastery. Genpo Sherab Tsepal said, "We should build at Tengboche."

Chatang Chothar and many others agreed. As some Sherpas suggested other places, they went to Rongbuk again to ask Ngawang Tenzin Norbu. The high lama replied, "At Tengboche, on the point at the edge of the flat area."

Ngawang Tenzin Norbu

When they were ready to build the first sponsors were Genpo Sherab Tsepal, Lama Karma and Thakdo Kunzang. All the local Sherpas helped with the construction that started in 1916 and took three years.

Ngawang Tenzin Norbu came for the opening celebration. The Mani Rimdu dances started at that time and have continued ever since. When Ngawang Tenzin Norbu was here, so many Sherpas came that he gave teachings.

In old Tengboche gompa: statue of Ngawang Tenzin Norbu, reliquary and statue of Lama Gulu.

Four tawa came from Dzamtra, near Thame, and later the number of monks increased. Everything went well with the monastery for eighteen years.

At that time, the Ranas controlled Nepal. Their chief Biman Samshar heard Chatang Chothar built a monastery at Tengboche, so he sent money and food for the monks.

Fourteen years later, Biman Samshar's son came to visit Tengboche. As he reached the entry stupa, a powerful earthquake took place and the delegation returned. That morning it had been very difficult to open the lock of the gompa. All the monks had been out to greet the Rana son, so no one was hurt when the earthquake happened.

During the earthquake the rear end of the gompa's roof collapsed. The front end where the statues were and where Chatang Chothar was sitting did not collapse. The disaster did not injure him, but, later that evening Chatang Chothar quietly passed away in a little house behind the gompa.

These events overwhelmed the tawas so they went to visit Ngawang Tenzin Norbu. He replied that they must build the monastery again, that it would be even better than before and explained the importance of having monasteries. This high lama then donated some money for rebuilding the monastery.

Ngawang Gelgen, a monk otherwise called *Umze Gelgen*, was mostly responsible for rebuilding the monastery. The other tawas and Sherpas also helped. At the start of the work was a very good sign; a carpenter from Lhasa arrived here. He knew how to survey and properly construct gompas. He did his best to make the entire building very sound. When the building was complete, the artist *Kappa Kalden* painted the insides. He was so skilled, that for many years the colors and surfaces of the paintings still looked very good. From the good work of these two individuals, many people thought Tengboche's was the best gompa.

Tengboche has become a symbol of the peace and beauty in Nepal, especially for tourism. We have the small hydro electricity plant that provides power to all the houses and lodges in Tengboche. The electricity was sponsored by the King Mahendra Trust and the American Himalayan Foundation.

Tengboche Rinpoche's Story

Tengboche Rinpoche, the Abbot of the monastery, is teacher and counselor on matters as varied as health, politics, the naming of children, education and building bridges. People regard him as a high lama because he studied at monastic universities in Tibet and is the reincarnation of Chatang Chothar, the monastery's founder. The term, *rinpoche*, is a title bestowed on very special teachers and reincarnate lamas. Tengboche Rinpoche is deeply committed to the development of Nepal and is active on committees to help the local people and to preserve the Sherpa culture.

I was born in Namche in 1935. At that time, there were forests all around and not many people. Pangboche, Phortse, Khunde, Khumjung and Thame all existed before Namche. Slowly, people from Khumjung, of the *Paldorje* clan, moved to Namche starting potato fields and building houses. It became the main center on the trade route to Tibet and people moved there from Tibet and from lower villages. Namche grew, but there was no *gompa* here. Then Dzamtra lama, born in Thame of the Shangku clan, in 1905 built the Namche *mani lha-khang* (big prayer wheel). In 1910, Namche gompa was established. This is my homeland.

Tengboche Rinpoche

One of my ancestors came from Wolungchung district (near Kanchenjunga), through Tibet and settled in a place called Thome. This man, called Mingma, had a son, Lhondup, my grandfather. Passang Namgyal was my father.

My mother Palzim Dickie, came from the Shangku clan in Thame. She moved to Namche when she married my father.

Passang Namgyal came here to Tengboche to receive *whang* (long life blessing) from Chatang Chothar (Lama Gulu) A month later, the lama passed away and my father was the last person to receive whang from him. That must be why my father had a very strong and healthy life until the age of 92.

When I was born they gave me the name Passang Tenzin. My father went to Tibet and when he arrived at Kyabrok that night

C. von Furer-Haimendorf

Tengboche Rinpoche (1956)

had a dream about Kang Rinpoche (Mt. Kailash). The house owner heard the story next morning and said, "Your son must be a Sangchen Samphel Tulpa (a high reincarnate)." My father remained in Tibet doing business.

As a small child, I talked about wanting to go home to Tengboche. Meanwhile, my mother carried me to Lhasa and stayed with Genpo Sherab Tsepal, a sponsor of Tengboche. His wife was my father's aunt. When they saw me going to high seats and places and talking about Tengboche, the aunt had a dream about the previous Tengboche lama. They thought I might be his reincarnation. So, we all went to Rongbuk, to see the lama Zatul Ngawang Tenzin Norbu.

This high lama said, "This is the true Tengboche *tulku* (reincarnate)." He gave me the name Ngawang Tenzin Zangbu. Umze Gelgen, a monk at Rongbuk, was the previous lama's nephew. As we had arrived at Rongbuk, upon seeing him, I ran up to hug him, as if I had known him before. Everyone was satisfied.

We returned to Khumbu over the Nangpa La. Arriving in Namche, the monks had brought possessions of the previous lama, mixed in with other monks' belongings. I picked out everything that had belonged to the previous lama, Chatang Chothar. Everyone agreed, and I came to Tengboche at the age of five, to be raised as the Reincarnate Lama and Abbot of the monastery.

When I was about six, I had to go to Kathmandu for a smallpox vaccination. Upon returning to Tengboche, I learned to read and studied some religion. Another trip to Kathmandu followed.

At the age of nine, I was taken over the Nangpa La to Gyantse Lingbu, a small, very good monastery in Tibet. A lama by the name of Lha-chen Jigdel Tenzin Pawo, from the king of Sikkim's clan, taught me the Mindroling teachings of the Nyingmapa sect. After learning Minling Thartse and more religion, I took vows from this lama. I spent three years in Gyantse; studying and doing prostrations. While there, my guardian, Umze Gelgen, passed away.

Then, I went to Talung Chib-phug, a Karmapa monastery, near Lhasa. I met two famous lamas, the 16th Gyalwa Karmapa Rigpe Dorje and Situ Pema Whangchuk Gyalpo, who taught religion and gave an initiation that prepared me for further studies. After Chib-phug monastery, I visited the Lhasa Jokang, the Potala, and Sera, Drebung, and Ganden monasteries.

After I returned to Gyantse, my teacher, Lha-chen Jigdel Tenzin Pawo passed away while visiting Lhasa. So, two months later, I went to Tsedhong Cho-de near Shigatse. There, under Ngor Kanchen Ngawang Lodo Samphel Nyingpo, I completely studied the Lamde Cho, teachings of the Sakyapa sect. In the winter, I went to a place called Tanag Thubten Namgyel near Shigatse.

The next spring, I came back to live at Tengboche. A few years later, I returned to Tibet to visit Sange Tenzin and Dudjom Rinpoche, at Samye monastery. I studied religion in Tibet for five more years. At the age of twenty, I had an initiation and teachings for about a month with Jamyang Khentse Choki Lodro. Four years later, I studied with Khentse Rinpoche in Kalimpong for three months.

I have received four awards from the King of Nepal, including the medal, Ghorka Duchin Bau, fourth. In the fall of 1983, I visited Tibet after many years, as part of an official Nepalese delegation. The next year I helped prepare and host a visit to Nepal by lamas still living in Tibet.

Reconstruction of Tengboche's Gompa

Reconstruction of Tengboche monastery's gompa started after the fire of January 19, 1989. The monastery itself was first established in 1916 and the gompa has been built or rebuilt now three times. The total strength of monks fluctuates and at present we have forty.

During the year of the fire, I personally observed several bad omens. In the

Reconstruction of gompa (1991)

mountains it snowed in an unusual way and there was unrest in political affairs. Moreover, unusual events in Mustang destroyed several houses by snow avalanches.

The fire at Tengboche monastery happened because the monk in-charge of operating the electric switches in the gompa had gone to Namche. During his absence, another monk went to put on the lights and accidentally used the wrong switch that turned on the room heater in the middle of the monastery office. The office was full of paper scrolls for a new prayer wheel.

The fire spread from that room through the wooden floor to the entire building. It went through the whole night. Monks, villagers and trekkers spotted fire going in the monastery and came and tried their best to save the gompa's treasures from the fire. Though people could not stop the fire, they rescued some invaluable statues, books and *thankas* (paintings) from the burning building. Due to the shortage of people on the spot, we lost numerous valuable old treasures. Villagers nearby ran through the night to the site and were able to prevent the destruction of the monk's homes.

The next morning, people from Namche, Khunde, Khumjung, Phortse and Pangboche came here. It was a big shock and disappointment to see what had happened at Tengboche Monastery.

At the time of the devastation, I was in Kathmandu. I flew to Tengboche on January 21, 1989, for about an hour to see the destruction. A week later, I went from Kathmandu to Bhutan with the *ku-dung* (casket) of the late Holiness Dudjom Rinpoche. I was there for one week and on the way back to Kathmandu met Sir Edmund Hillary. He visited Tengboche the day I returned from Bhutan and saw the ruins of the gompa. We had a long conversation about the monastery's gompa and the program for its reconstruction.

I started the Tengboche Gompa Reconstruction Committee with Sherpa people in Kathmandu. We forwarded the news of devastation to His Majesty King Birendra and to several other administrative people.

We could not start reconstruction that same year, because it was a *lo-nak* (black, inauspicious year). We were able to start collecting donations for the construction. We also received a donation of NRs 1,00,000 from the

Solu-Khumbu District HQ. During that year, we collected rock and wood for the construction and cleared the site of the ruins.

Finally, reconstruction began on April 5, 1990, an auspicious day to commence. We placed *sachok pumba* (sacred vases to bury in the ground) in the important places on the site where we would build the gompa. On that day we had several guests including Sir Edmund Hillary's son Peter, officers from the National Park in Namche and administrative members from Namche Bazaar. On April 27, 1990, people from every part of Khumbu, Sir Edmund, Zeke O'Connor and National Park staff came to Tengboche gompa to celebrate the beginning of the gompa reconstruction. In this ceremony we placed the corner stones in the foundation. It was very important to do the proper pujahs as we placed the stones in the specific places.

The stone that we used for building monastery was dug from the backside of monastery. At first, we did not expect that rock would be enough for us to build the whole gompa. Eventually it made plenty of stone to complete the gompa and we did not have to carry in any stones from anywhere else. During the whole construction period, we did not have any problems. Nature also favored us by providing clear weather and moreover, we did not have any water shortages.

We finished the outer part of the wall of the main part on December 1990 and in the following year we finished building the front courtyard (*deng*) and put the wooden paneling inside the gompa. The late Mrs. Busak of Germany helped us obtain volumes of the Ka-gyur and Tengyur from Tibet.

We did several pujahs during the construction of the gompa. There are very specific pujahs done at each stage of building a gompa. As usual, we also performed Mani Rimdu festival.

The skilled sculpture artists arrived on March 25, 1992, and started their work, completing four smaller statues of deities. They started to make the fifteen- foot tall statue of the Buddha on July 1, 1992.

We started painting the interior on September 4, 1992. We put a tin roof on the gompa then the following year replaced it with the copper roof. Finally, the roof, interior finishing and statues were

new Manjushri statue

completed in 1993. All the major work on the gompa was done and just the wall murals and small jobs remained unfinished.

On September 17, 1993, His Holiness Tulshi Rinpoche came to Tengboche from Thubten Cholling monastery for the pujah consecrating the completion of the new gompa. The pujah lasted from 19 to 22 of September. Tulshi Rinpoche stayed for 11 days. On completion of the pujah we had many different visitors come for the opening ceremony. Our distinguished guests were Prime Minister Koirala of Nepal, Sir Edmund Hillary of the Himalayan Trust, representatives from the German and Japanese embassies and our patron from Switzerland who donated the brass roof, Mr. Tanner. People from all over Khumbu came and made the inauguration day bright and full of life. We are proud to say that at last our gompa rises up again with the help from many people in Khumbu, Nepal and around the world.

Description of Tengboche Gompa

The old *gompa* (temple) at Tengboche was very famous around the world. Everyone will always remember it for its special appearance and the quality of its paintings. The lower room of a gompa is the *dus-khang*, where the monks gather. Here, the main statue at the front was Sakyamuni, the Buddha. To his right was Chenrezig, the god of compassion, and to his left Ogyen Rinpoche (another name for Guru Rinpoche). On both sides of these statues were texts of the Ka-gyur printed in Narthang, Tibet. Above the Ka-gyur, were Nyingma Gyubum texts printed in Derge, Kham. These are important texts regarding meditation.

Ser-sang Lha-khang of old gompa

There were several handwritten *Boom* texts and one set written in silver and gold. This set was originally from a house in Thame but someone took it to Darjeeling to sell. A Sherpa nun found the books, bought them and brought this set of Boom texts to Tengboche. These texts were rescued from the fire and are all intact.

The statue on the right wall was of Arya Maitreya, the coming Buddha, and on both sides of it were the volumes of the Ten-gyur. The wall to the left beside the door had a rare mural of the Minling Maha-kala Lhatsok, an incarnation of Chenrezig that is a fierce protector of Buddhism. A curtain usually hid this mural so only those people with the proper preparations could see it. On the ceiling was a painting of nine mandalas. The west side had windows and murals.

On the porch (*go-chor*) of the *dus-khang* were murals of Jomo Miyo Lang Sangma, Khumbila, and of the protective deities of *gompas*. There were also stones with Lama Sangwa Dorje's footprints and a rock from which he fed his dog. These stones survived the fire and are now outside the front entrance of the gompa.

The upper floor, the Ser-sang Lha-khang (gold-copper-god-house) had many statues specially relating to Tengboche and the Nyingmapa sect. The books here were the Rinchen Tertzu, the collection of all Nyingmapa *terma* (sacred texts). Here were also many other texts, more than 300 in all. All the walls were painted with murals.

A small room on the right side of this one was the *mahakal-khang* (room of the protectors) that is mainly for Turto Lhamu, a female protectress. Only the Tengboche monks were allowed into this shrine. On this floor, there were two other small rooms with very good murals. On the very top floor is the *u-khang* with the painting of the *tertugyazo*, 100 forms of Guru Rinpoche's disciples with special spiritual powers.

The new gompa has been built to look similar to the old one on the outside. However we took the opportunity of the reconstruction to make the courtyard and storage rooms of the gompa larger to provide more space for the monks' activities. The inside of the new gompa is different.

The main statue in the do-khang is the fifteen-foot high image of the Sakyamuni Buddha. On either side of him are Manjushri, the god of wisdom, and Maitreya, the future Buddha. The volumes of the Ken-gyur are on the sides. The wall paintings will eventually be done and show details of the life of the Buddha. Upstairs in the Ser-sang Lha-khang is the *ku-dung* (reliquary) of Lama Gulu. The volumes of the Ten-gyur are here as

statue hands in **mudra**

are the texts special to the Nyingmapa sect, the Rinchen Tertzu. A statue of Guru Rinpoche is in the room next to the Ser-sang Lha-khang.

The courtyard outside the gompa is called the *cham-ra*. On its right is the *rhung-khang*, the kitchen. Outside, around the main building, are the monk's houses. On the west and north sides of the *gompa* are the cultural center, the student's hostel and the new school building.

Tawas (Monks) and Duties in the Monastery

Monks study, teach and perform religious rites for the Sherpa community. As well, they must help with the monastery's work, as stewards, custodians, or prayer leaders.

Students enter the school at Tengboche at the age of seven. Their families pay a fee for their tuition and accommodation in the student hostel.

Not all *tawas* are *lamas*. This title is reserved for religious teachers, whether or not they have taken vows of celibacy. Women may also study and take vows to become *anis* (nuns). Communities of *anis* live at Devuche, Thamo and Pangboche.

All the *tawas* (monks) at Tengboche are Sherpas. Some became tawas at seven years of age. First, they learn to read and write Tibetan. Then there are many different subjects to learn such as religion, history, psychology and medicine, but each student studies at his own pace.

There are three levels of vows of commitment to the monastery: *genyan*, with 5 rules which are similar to those of a lay practitioner; *getsup*, with 10 main rules; and *gelong*, with 250 rules. To take the final *gelong* vows and become a *tawa*, a man must be celibate and at least 20 years old. He then lives in his own house at the monastery. *Tawas* are usually supported by their families who consider it an honor to have a *tawa* in the family.

Gradually the monks may work up to being *umze* (prayer leader), then *loben* (in charge of the monks). Those who aren't proficient students do work for the monastery getting wood, selling campsites, shopping, or serving tea. It takes at least 17 years to complete all the monastery duties by a rotation the monks determine by turn and discussion.

The Teachings at Tengboche

The religion of Tengboche is the Nyingmapa sect of Tibetan Buddhism, the oldest sect because the teachings came directly from Guru Rinpoche. The main descriptions of the gompa's name, the pujahs done and the statues come from the Ogyen Mindroling teachings. The Mindroling college gave rise to Rongbuk monastery and then Tengboche. Most of the books at these monasteries came from the Mindroling college.

Mindroling was a Nyingmapa college in Tibet founded by *terdak lingpa* Gyurme Dorje Pema Karwang. Jamgon Kongtrul Ladro Thaye collected the Rinchen Tertzu texts. The term *terdak lingpa* used in titles of books and ceremonies means that they follow the way of a teacher who was a *terton.*

The Ceremonies of Tengboche Gompa

Lhosar, the Tibetan new year is celebrated from the first to the third day of the Sherpa first month. Then from the 5th to 10th the monks do Tsedub Yangnyig Kundu for long life, where they distribute blessings and relics to *tawas* and *anis* (nuns).

On the 3rd day of the third month, the Hammogang Lhapsang worships the god of the ridge facing the gompa. Lhapsang is an offering of incense to the gods for protection. Burning *shugpa* (juniper) is refreshing to the gods and indicates whom they are to protect.

During the monsoon, from the fifteenth of the fifth month to the thirtieth of the sixth month is *yarnay*, the summer retreat. During this retreat, the monks don't leave the monastery and do prayers every morning.

From the first to eleventh days of the seventh month, the monks perform Vajra Satva, which finishes with a

Hammogang lhapsang

jinsak, a fire pujah. This is a pujah to Vajrasattva, the god of spiritual power, for the forgiveness of sin so that peace may prevail. For this pujah they also make a sand mandala, which is rarely done in Nepal.

Mani Rimdu is celebrated from the first to the eighteenth of the ninth month. It is described in the next chapter.

Kangso Dupa, where all the gods are worshipped, is performed from the 23rd to the 29th of the tenth month. The monks do this pujah for protection, because if we do not thank the gods, then they may be offensive. *Kang* means fulfill, *so* means to mend or to purify.

At the end of each year, the monks perform Gu-tor to prevent problems in the past year caused by demons.

On the 15th day of every month, the full moon, the monks do Sojong, with special meditation in the morning. During this time, they meet to talk about how they might have hurt each other. It is a time for confession and conciliation between the *tawas*.

Every day the monks gather for *mang ja* (salt tea) and to do a short pujah. The monks also gather to do Shitro, *tsog*, or special *pujahs* requested by villagers, the monastery, or the monks themselves.

Buddhist Education at Tengboche School

Once in northern Nepal, lamas came from Tibet establishing many gompas. However until 27 years ago, people traditionally went to Tibet for a higher Buddhist education. There, higher studies were available at all of the monasteries. Many returned to Nepal to do the work of the gompas, while others though they wanted to be in Nepal, stayed in Tibet because the facilities were better. Now since the situation in Tibet has changed, we cannot go there to study and it is difficult to obtain a religious education. Now it is very important that we establish our own schools here in Nepal.

There have been no Buddhist schools in the mountains until now, so I once started a school here at Tengboche. We have had problems maintaining the school since the fire, but hope to resume having a school now that we finished the new gompa. This school at Tengboche is very important.

People in many areas of Nepal's mountains will then think about starting Buddhist schools in their areas. One benefit of the schools is that they help preserve the Himalayan culture, so fewer people will move away and the villages will be able to improve and develop. For this reason, the Tengboche school is very important for our culture.

The subjects taught at Buddhist schools are the Himalayan alphabet, reading and writing, grammar, literature and teaching from the *Sutra* and *Tantra.* Other subjects may the Hindi-Sanskrit language, religious books, medicine, old stories, chanting and philosophy. As well, the students have religious duties like learning and helping with pujahs, making *tormas,* playing instruments and studying meditation. They will study meditation until they are 30 or 40 years old when they will begin to practice it.

In the near future, we will search for three very good teachers. One will teach the alphabet, another will teach reading and the third will supervise the students. A little later, we will teach the students proper Nepali, then English so that they will be able to explain our religion and culture to foreigners. We also hope to be able to teach traditional Tibetan medicine, and making clay statues and thankas.

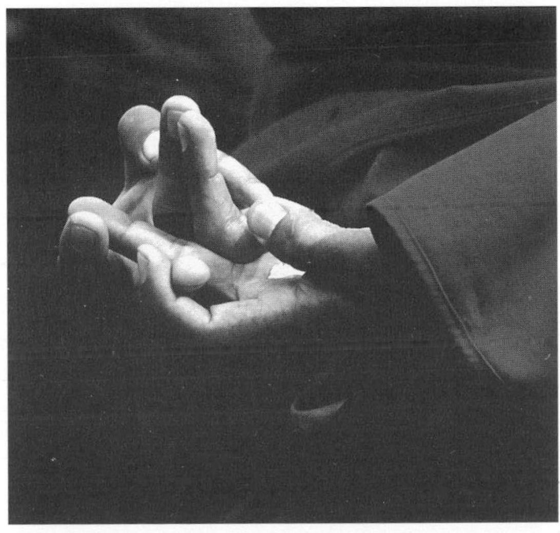

Mudra *(hand position) of offering*

Procession for Mani Rimdu blessing day.

Chapter Nine

Mani Rimdu Festival

Mani Rimdu Festival

The festive days of Mani Rimdu celebrate the completion of ten days of prayers for the benefit of all beings.

The Story and Purpose of Mani Rimdu

The main purpose of Mani Rimdu is the prayers which worship Phakpa Chenrezig, the god of compassion. His blessing brings peace and good fortune to everyone. During Mani Rimdu we invoke Phakpa Chenrezig's blessing on the *rilbu,* the long-life-pills, and perform the dances which showing former times worship this deity.

Main Rimdu is a fairly recent tradition in Khumbu. For the opening ceremony of the Tengboche, Zatul Ngawang Tenzin Norbu of Rongbuk came to consecrate the monastery and the monks performed the dances here for the first time then. Since that event, Mani Rimdu continues at the same time of year. It used to be in the tenth month, but that was very cold for spectators and because of bad weather, difficult for preparations. Now, Mani Rimdu is held in the ninth month, unless a double month shifts it to the tenth.

Each sect and monastery have their own style of dancing. The dances at Tengboche came from Rongbuk. Before the Chinese came, these particular dances were done at Rongbuk, and started at Tengboche. Later, the lama at Chiwong gompa in Solu started Mani Rimdu there. When Thame became established as a celibate monastery, they started performing Mani Rimdu there also. It is held in the ninth month at Tengboche, tenth month at Chiwong and fourth month at Thame. There is no other identical Mani Rimdu anywhere else in Tibet.

When Ngawang Tenzin Norbu started Rongbuk, the Mani Rimdu ceremony there was also small but after more and more *tawas* came, they decided to have the dancing. They copied dances from other Nyingmapa gompas in Tibet and added some new dances that Ngawang Tenzin Norbu created.

In Tibet, this kind of festival is performed mostly in the fifth month, with the dances on the 10th day. It is called Tse Chu, and is the most important one of the year. A small Tse Chu is done on the tenth day of every month.

Almost every monastery has their own style of doing dancing, at different times of the year and special days of the month. The many different kinds of dances came from the many different movements described in the *tantras*. The Buddhist Newars also perform dances that came from the Tantra scriptures.

There are monasteries in other areas of Nepal such as Mustang, where they also do dancing, however the dancing is done only for a short time, not all day.

The name Mani Rimdu comes from *mani* the chant for Phakpa Chenrezig, *ril* the little red pellets and *dub* the blessing on the *rilbu*.

The blessing for the *rilbu* goes back to when Guru Rinpoche brought religion to Tibet. As well as Nyingma-kama, which he taught directly to the people, there was Nyingma-terma, which were teachings in books hidden for the future. Guru Rinpoche foretold that a time would come when wars and hard times would make the books necessary. The people who found these books are the *Tertons*.

One of these, Tertak Lingba, whose full name was Gyurme Dorje Pema Karwang, found a hidden book called Thuje Chenpo Deshe Kundu. This book belongs to the Ogyen Mindroling college of the Nyingmapa sect and is read for Mani Rimdu. The Tibetan name Thuje Chenpo means Maha-karuna in Sanskrit, which translates as great compassion. Deshe Kundu is the specific name of this book. Thuje Chenpo is also a name used for Jigten

Making sand mandala

Wangchuk, the main aspect of Phakpa Chenrezig worshipped during the Mani Rimdu pujah.

This book is mostly about *drubchen*, a very powerful pujah body to invoke Phakpa Chenrezig.

Mani Rimdu starts on the first day of the ninth month with Sa-chog, the earth pujah to the gods of the four directions that consecrates the place where the pujah will take place. Thig-kor, the preparations of making torma and using colored sand to make the mandala, called the Dul-tson Kyil-khor begin the same day and continue until the fourth day.

From the fifth to the fourteenth days, the monks do the pujah called Ngo Zhi Cho-pa, that goes all day and night. In the morning the main pujah is to the action aspect of Phakpa Chenrezig, Lhachen Wangchuk, and then to the god Maha-kala, the protector of the Buddhist faith. Pujahs to other gods are done by turn, three one day, then three the next.

Jinsak, the fire ritual.

For the *whang*, on the fifteenth day, people come for the lama's blessing and to receive the *rilbu*. On the sixteenth day, the monks worship Phakpa Chenrezig by dancing. There are sixteen dances. The dances aim to prevent interference, accidents, impediments, change of mind, faith, or hindrance by sin. The seventeenth day concludes with *jinsak*, a fire pujah.

The Blessing Ceremony

On the fifteenth morning, the *tawas* receive a blessing themselves and in the afternoon people come for the lama's blessing and to receive the *rilbu*.

There are many kinds of *whangs*, blessings, and this is a *tor whang*. Many *torma* have been made for the *whang*, in pyramids representing mandalas. During the *whang*, Rinpoche and the *tawas* visualize a mandala that cleanses the sins of the people so they may gain merit. They distribute the *rilbu* over which the *mani* has been chanted. The *rilbu* are *chelab*, pills that generally cure or make the path after life a little easier. These *rilbu* contain relics from Guru Rinpoche's *ter* (spiritual treasures) that will bless our bodies.

The Cham (Masked Dances)

On the sixteenth day, are the dances that worship Phakpa Chenrezig. Each dance relates to a pujah done during the previous days.

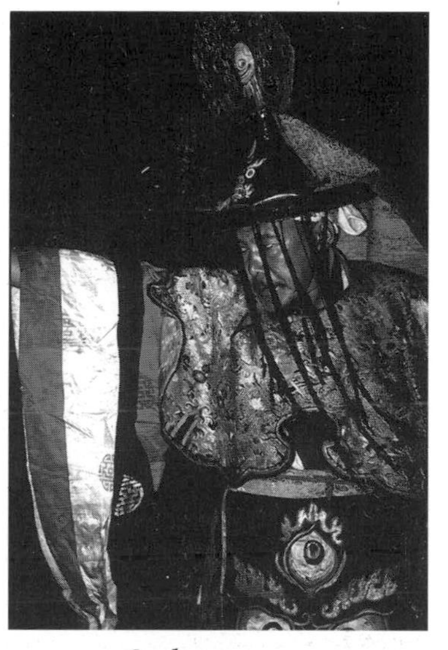

Serkyem

The dances come from when Guru Rinpoche blessed Samye, the first monastery in Tibet. He pretended to be his favorite god by imitating its body and danced the blessing. Since then, some lamas think they will see these dances in Dewachen. *Cham* means sacred dance.

There are many gods in Tibet who used to wear these costumes. The black hats were the costumes of the Phembu gods. Then it became the dress of the original *ngagpas* (married lamas) when they did the *thu-duph*, a powerful pujah. Later it became the dancing dress of monks and *ngagpas*.

Rol-cham is the grand entrance of the monks wearing yellow hats and playing pujah instruments.

Serkyem is the first dance with dancers wearing costumes and black hats. This dance invokes *tse gyepa* (improving one's life, longevity, appearance health and intelligence), *whang* (providing spiritual power) and *thub* (the ability to fight bad spirits). The black hats represent *ngagpa* or Vajrayana priests capable of using spiritual powers.

Ging-cham is the dance by four attendants of *Dorje Trollo.* Two females carry *nga* (drums) and two males carry *buk-chal* (cymbals). They make offerings of *tsog* to Dorje Trollo.

(Guru) Dorje Trollo

Guru Dorje Trollo is a single masked dancer representing one of the fierce forms of Guru Rinpoche. He is preceded by monks playing instruments.

Nga-cham originated as Guru Rinpoche's dance when he blessed Samye gompa. The six dancers wear golden hats with peacock feathers and carry drums. In the past Tibetan officials wore the golden hat.

Durdag-cham is a complicated dance with two skeletons and two black-hat dancers. The skeletons carry a dough figure, representing evil, on a rope between them. It is symbolically destroyed by the black-hat dancers.

Mi Tsering, the long life man, is a comic interlude.

The Maha-kala dance has eight characters all representing different deities; Tseringma (the main long-life sister), Maha-kala (the protector), and Maha-deva (Lhachen Whangchuk) are the main ones.

Zurra-rakye, a local protective god, carries a goat horn and long stick. Two *minaks* (attendants) accompany him. He is the guardian of Khenpalung, a hidden valley that has not yet been opened.

Khaadro are five female deities of wisdom often referred to as the sky-dancers.

Thog-den makes an appearance in the second comic dance. This

Tseringma

Zurra-rakye

Mi Tsering

is the only dance with any speaking as he jokes with his assistant or the crowd and teaches religion.

Maha-deva

Lhagma has the purpose of getting rid of left over rilbu, long life pills. Two masked dancers, one male and one female, perform this task.

Ti-jum is a *cham* where four masked dancers carry knives.

Zor-cham is a ritual exorcism in which dancers wearing black-hats carry small torma, *lok-par*, that signify evil. The dancers throw out these *torma*.

Then-cham also functions to get rid of evil. Half of the dancers wear black-hats, the other half masks.

Log -cham is the finale with some dancers from each cham.

For the different gods, there are different ways of praying, chanting or dancing that help make the gods closer to the dancer, and eventually a part of him, helping everyone. Sometimes, from prayers, deep thinking or meditation, the same happens. This makes the country peaceful and in the future will help everyone.

The lotus flower is a symbol of purity.

Glossary

Abbot - one who can transmit monastic vows. Also, a person who has attained a high degree of knowledge of Dharma and is authorized to teach.

Amphu Latse- pass from Khumbu to valleys to the southeast.

Ani- a Buddhist nun.

Avalokiteshvara – (Skt.) the sublime bodhisattva personifying the compassion of the Buddhas; also referred to as Lokeshvara, and Phakpa Chenrezig (Tib.).

Bardo - an intermediary state between death and subsequent rebirth.

Beyul- a sanctuary from the troubled world originally set aside by Guru Rinpoche.

Bodhisattva – 1. One who through compassion strives to attain full enlightenment for the sake of all beings. 2. One who has attained one of the levels of realization on the path to becoming a Buddha. 3. A sublime personification of a particular quality (compassion, wisdom, etc.) of enlightenment.

Buddha - the Fully Awakened One, a being who has removed the emotional and cognitive veils and is endowed with all enlightened qualities of realization. The historical Buddha lived over 2500 years ago.

Buddha Tsenchen - historical lama 370 years ago, father of three lamas who founded first Khumbu village gompas.

Cham - religious dance.

Chang-ter - texts hidden by Guru Rinpoche in Tibet.

Chatang Chothar - founder of Tengboche monastery, also called **Lama Gulu**.

Chenrezig - other Tibetan name for **Phakpa Chenrezig**, Avalokiteshvara.

Cho- Sherpa Buddhist religion.

Chorten (Tib.) (Skt. - **Stupa**) - a monument symbolizing the Buddha's enlightenment.

Dakini - The representation of wisdom in female form.

Deity (Tib.- **Lha**, Skt.- **Deva**)- this term designates a buddha or wisdom deity, sometimes a dharma protector (such as Khumbila). May also refer to the personifications of enlightenment (such as Phakpa Chenrezig).

Dharma - Sanskrit term used to indicate the doctrine of the Buddha.

Emptiness (Skt.- **Shunyata**) - the ultimate nature of phenomena (namely their lack of inherent existence) beyond the four spiritual extremes.

Enlightenment – the state of purification of all obscurations and realization of all qualities such as wisdom and compassion.

Gompa- the temple in village or monastery.

Gonpo - a principal protector.

Guru Rinpoche- established Buddhism in Tibet over 1250 years ago, also **Ogyen Rinpoche** or **Padma Sambhava.**

Hinayana - the fundamental teachings of Buddhist thought and practice. The motivation of Hinayana is generally for one's own liberation.

Indrabodhi - the king of Ogyen who discovered **Guru Rinpoche** as a child in an enormous lotus flower.

Jigten Whangchuk - other name for Avalokiteshvara, the deity personifying compassion.

Jomo Miyo Lung Sangma - goddess residing on Mt. Everest. Also called **Jomolungma** and **Chomolungma.**

Ka-gyur - collection of the volumes of the teachings of the Buddha.

Karuna – (Skt.) compassion.

Kham-Salmo-Gang - district of eastern Tibet from which the Sherpas came.

Khumbila - protective deity of Khumbu. Also called **Khumbu-Yul-Lha** (Khumbu-country-deity).

Kor - Buddhist text with variety of subjects.

Kyil-khor - mandala in Tibetan.

Lama (Skt. - **Guru**) - a highly realized spiritual teacher teacher and guide. A lama need not be a monk (tawa) and only a few monks are lamas. It is sometimes used as a polite way to address a monk.

Lha- god, deity.

Lhachen Whangchuk - Mahadeva, a protector representing the action form of **Chenrezig**.

Lha-khang - "god's house", a the main room of a temple or an altar.

Lhapsang - prayers by Sherpas to specified god.

Maha-deva - a proctector representing the action form of **Chenrezig**, "great god".

Maha-kala - a wrathful protector deity of Buddhism.

Mahayana - the tradition of Buddhism practised in China, Japan, Korea, Mongolia, Tibet, and the Himalayan regions. It aims to attain enlightenment for all beings and promotes universal compassion to deliver all beings from suffering and its causes. The **Vajrayana** is a branch of the Mahayana.

Mandala (Skt.) (Tib. kyil khor) – a spiritual diagram of the center and circumference. 1. The circular space of an enlightened being at the center that is visualized during Buddhist practices. 2. A diagram of the visualized ideal universe as an offering. An offering mandala is the arrangement of an offering, or is visualized, such as when a practitioner offers the entire universe.

Manjushri - the personification of the body aspect and wisdom of all the Buddhas.

Mantra - syllables that when recited protects the mind of the practitioner from delusion and invokes the particular deity in the form of sound.

Merit - positive energy arising from wholesome action or virtue.

Mindroling - Nyingmapa college in Tibet.

Mudra - a ritual gesture performed with the hands.

Nangpa La – the pass between Khumbu and Tibet.

Ngagpa- lay lama, minister.

Ngawang Tenzin Norbu - founder of Rongbuk monastery in Tibet.

Nirvana - the state beyond suffering. In the Mahayana, buddhahood transcends both suffering and the peace of nirvana.

Nyingmapa – the original sect of Tibetan Buddhism, also called the "Old Translation School". The followers of the first teachings translated and taught in Tibet.

Ogyen Rinpoche - **Guru Rinpoche**.

Padmasambhava - literally lotus-born. Also called **Guru Rinpoche** who was predicted by the Buddha as the one who would teach the Vajrayana. He was invited to Tibet in the eighth century and succeeded in establishing the Buddhist teachings.

Phachin - first Sherpa to come to Khumbu.

Phakpa Chenrezig – the sublime bodhisattva (deity) personifying the compassion of the Buddhas. Also called Avalokiteshvara or **Lokeshvara** in Skt.

Phug - cave.

Rinpoche - title for high lamas and reincarnates.

Rongbuk - monastery on north side of Everest.

Ru - Sherpa clans, "bones".

Sangwa Dorje – lama who founded Pangboche gompa and Dumje festival over 350 years ago.

Sanskrit - ancient language of India. Many words are Sanskrit, abbreviated Skt.

Shakyamuni - historical Buddha who attained full enlightenment about twenty-five hundred years ago.

Sherpa - literally sher-pa means east-people.

Shitro - meditational deities in peaceful or wrathful forms and representing different aspects of one's buddha-nature.

Shuenya - wisdom, perception.

Stupa (Skt.) (Tib.- **Chorten**) - a monument symbolizing the Buddha's enlightenment. Stupas are the most typical Buddhist monuments and are found in a variety of forms in all Buddhist countries. They often contain the relics of enlightened beings or lamas.

Sur - food burnt on coals and offered to spirits, especially of deceased family members, who are able to consume only the smell of burnt food.

Tawa - monk.

Ten-gyur - the translation of the commentaries on the Buddha's discourses.

Terma - literally "treasures". Guru Rinpoche, and others, concealed teachings and sacred objects to be found in later times, when they would benefit the world and its inhabitants. He concealed the treasure teachings deep in the minds of his disciples, who were themselves accomplished practitioners. The teachings were often connected to certain physical objects, such as scrolls of texts. In the relevant historical period, the discovery of the objects often prompted the reincarnates of the disciples to reveal the treasure teachings received centuries before from the Guru. The collection of terma forms one of the main sources of teaching and practice of the Nyingma school.

Terton – a discoverer of texts hidden by Guru Rinpoche and others in the early years of Buddhism in Tibet.

Torma - a ritual object, often modeled from tsampa and butter, which can symbolize a deity, a mandala , an offering , or occasionally a weapon to fight negative forces.

Tsampa - flour made from roasted barley or other grains. A staple food in Tibet.

Tso - offerings of cooked rice.

Tulku – a recognized incarnation of a lama, who is usually found in childhood and brought up to inherit the lineage and monastery of their predecessor.

Vajra - diamond weapon, a symbol of indestructibility, used to represent skilful means or compassion. The vajra (Tib.- **dorje**) is used in rituals in conjunction with a bell (**trilbu**) that symbolizes the wisdom of emptiness.

Vajrayana - the "diamond vehicle" practice that uses special techniques for a quicker but more difficult path to enlightenment.

Whang - blessing ceremony.

Wisdom - the ability to correctly understand emptiness and the nature of the mind.

Yidam - a deity representing different aspects of enlightenment. Yidams may be peaceful or wrathful, and are meditated upon according to the nature and needs of the individual practitioner.

Map of Khumbu Valley

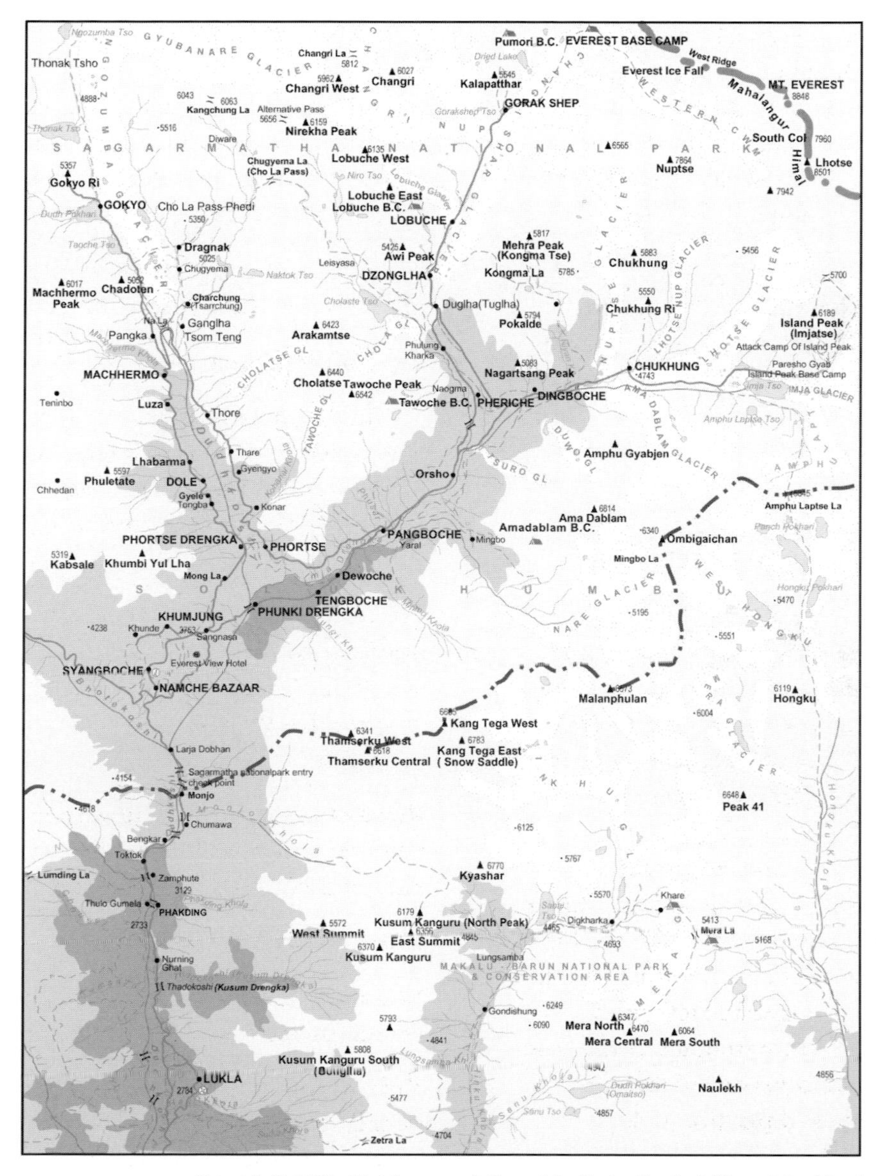

Mani stone with deities symbolizing wisdom, compassion, and spiritual power.